Rede Children's Ministry

IN THE 21ST CENTURY

Becky Fischer

511 S. Anderson St.
Bismarck, ND 58504

Dedication

This book is lovingly dedicated to Sister Violet Nichols. Sister Vi, as we called her, was the Sunday School superintendent of my dad's church when I was growing up and my childhood mentor from ages five to fourteen. She decided because I was the pastor's daughter, it was my duty to pray with all the new kids she brought to church for salvation and the baptism in the Holy Spirit, thus making me the first "kid in ministry" I ever knew. I have no idea how many boys and girls I prayed with during those years under her leadership, and neither of us had any inkling of the foundation she was laying in me for what I do today in children's ministry. When I was fourteen she went home to be with the Lord while kneeling at the altar of an annual vacation Bible School she was conducting for neighborhood children.

Table of Contents

Acknowledgments

The title of this book and the term I continually use throughout it was not original with me. The first time I heard the phrase "redefining children's ministry in the 21st century," I was reading a newsletter published by Lenny LaGuardia, head of the Children's Equipping Center at the International House of Prayer in Kansas City, MO. When I first read it, it captured my heart and my imagination. I have been using it ever since, because it so fully expresses what I carry in my heart as a vision for the body of Christ. Lenny told me he had been using the phrase for many years already. Small wonder since he has been one of the pioneers in this area of training children to walk in the supernatural. Thank you, Lenny, for loaning it to me for this book.

Sincere thanks also goes to Tim Carpenter, former Project Editor for CharismaLife Publishers, Daphne Kirk, author of Reconnecting the Generations, Esther Ilnisky, founder of the Esther Network and author of Let the Children Pray, and my Pastors Alan and Carol Koch from Lee's Summit, MO for taking time out of their busy schedules to read through my original manuscript, and give me their feedback, constructive criticism, and suggestions for improvement. These friends are wonderful ministers to both children and adults, and their input and individual perspectives were very valuable to the finished product you are holding in your hand.

Forward

The first time Becky came and ministered in our church she taught our children on the Glory of God. The Holy Spirit moved in amazing ways on our kids. Among other things, there were manifestations of gold dust on their hands. There were some children who were on their faces crying out to God in prayer, travailing for over an hour after the services. Some parents finally had to scoop their kids up off the floor and take them home. That's when we figured out that what Becky was teaching and her vision of bringing kids into the supernatural realm of God was the real thing. The days of flannelgraphs being the primary media of teaching children about the things of God is over, and releasing kids into ministry is ushering in a brand new day!

We have always taken our kids to one of the best Christian camps in the nation each summer. It could be compared to a Christian Disneyland with all the fun and toys, and exciting events that go on. Then one year we also drove them all the way to North Dakota to one of Becky's camps where the Holy Spirit moved in profound and powerful ways. We told our kids that we couldn't keep attending both camps, and they would have to choose one over the other. Every one of them without skipping a beat said, "We want to go back to North Dakota!" They picked the Presence over the toys.

We have had a relationship with Becky since the summer of 2003. It was an instant click, and an instant God-thing. We felt like when she came into our church, even though we had been training and teaching the kids prior to her coming, she had something on her that helped catapult our children to a higher level. We were then able to capture, maintain, and run with it in our children's ministry as a result. We have had all kinds of vacation Bible schools over the years, but we had never had anything that impacted and changed the lives of our boys and girls more than this ministry, the foundation of which is in taking kids into the realm of the supernatural. As a result of the impact, we started a children's intercessory prayer group, encompassing youngsters from ages five to eleven. It is still going strong and we have been able to not just maintain it, but also move it up even higher spiritually. Every time our kids come in contact with Becky and her unique ministry, they seem to get thrust a little deeper into the things of the Spirit.

Recently kids came from all over the country to our church to attend Becky's *School of Healing For Kids*, and she and her team taught the children on all aspects of healing. Even though our own kids already knew a lot of things about healing, they were still once again pushed up several levels spiritually. Boys and girls began ministering the last night of the conference as adults came in. People were getting healed everywhere. They were amazed because it was the kids who were calling out words of knowledge, and doing the praying for the sick. That was the goal. We want to push our kids above where we are. What has been our ceiling we want to become the floor for them.

So the message of this book is the real deal, and if you take it to heart, you will learn how to impart and mentor the next generation, which is what our families and our churches need. Our children need spiritual mothers and fathers who will impart and raise up the next generation. That is what this book is all about. We use the Kids in Ministry International material in our church from the nursery through out our children's ministry, and we know it works from first hand experience. We highly endorse what Becky shares in *Redefining Children's Ministry in the 21st Century*, because we know it will transform your children, and your children's ministry.

Pastors Alan and Carol Koch
Christ Triumphant Church
Lee's Summit, MO

Introduction

The entire premise and tone of this book is that we have a crisis in the modern and postmodern Church of Jesus Christ concerning ministry to children. Many in children's ministry already knew it. But once George Barna and The Barna Group came out with their findings on the subject and passed the information on to leaders of the Christian world, it shed some startling light on the situation that has given rise to new interest in how we should approach ministry to the smallest saints.

Barna published his findings in a book entitled *Transforming Children into Spiritual Champions*. If you have not already read it, I highly recommend you do so, then pass the copy on to your head pastor. It's a real wake-up call to the body of Christ concerning our children. Just before publishing this book Barna wrote another one called *Real Teens*. This also would be very beneficial for you to read, because it shows you where the kids we are currently teaching are headed if there's not a dramatic turn around in the strategy of the church world very soon. It also lets us see the fruit, or lack thereof, of what we have produced in the kids that have already passed through our children's ministries' doors within just the last few years. It's cause for serious reflection.

Having been in children's ministry since 1991, I have observed from first hand experience so much of what Barna shares, especially in areas where he reveals things like the number of thirteen-year-olds who still do not know what worship is, have never felt the presence of God, or to their knowledge have never heard His voice even after spending twelve years under our influence. In other words, somehow God has never been made real to them. We should not be surprised that they do not want to continue in church and religion where there is no life or relationship with their Creator. Kids hunger for the supernatural life we told them exists but which they've seldom if ever seen.

It is from this perspective that this book is crafted, based on my personal experiences and observations. The ideas I present are by no means original with me. There has always been a remnant of children's ministers who have trained kids to walk in the supernatural power of God. History is littered with examples of children who have preached, prophesied, prayed, healed the sick, led revivals, and more. In the last twenty-five to thirty years particularly there has been a growing number of children's ministers who have not only believed and taught what I present here, but also have far more exciting stories to tell than I do.

There have been tremendous ministers such as Helen Beason, Gwen Davis, Mark Harper, Lelonie Hibberd, Pete Hohmann, Bobby and Ginger Hussey, Esther Ilnisky, Daphne Kirk, Lenny LaGuardia, Jane Mackie, Jeanne Medaras, John Tasch, David Walters, and others known and unknown too numerous to mention who have led the way. They have made enormous strides in making the church world aware of how God wants to use children as His partners in ministry and have impacted the lives of multiplied thousands of children. It is on the shoulders of these pioneering men and women that I stand and take my place. Many of them were ones who greatly influenced me in what I do and the message I preach today.

But what is amazing and also frustrating as we consider all they have done and the years they've been doing it, is that their influence has not made any greater inroads into typical children's ministry in the widespread body of Christ. They are still the anomalies. It is for this very reason I felt compelled to write this book. It is my passion to see these principles and concepts become what I call **mainstream children's ministry** in my lifetime. As I say in a later chapter, it should be just as common to hear that a church has a children's prayer team, a children's evangelism team, a children's prophetic ministry team, a children's worship team, and children's healing team, as it is to hear they have a Sunday School. Our children need to be trained to walk in the power of the Holy Spirit at young ages. This is the foundation of a fulfilling, exciting Christian life-style.

Aggravating the problem of not making a more permanent, broader impact in the body of Christ with this message is the constant high turn-over of children's ministers in local churches. Just about the time one leader goes to a conference, hears this vision, and starts to implement new ideas, it seems they leave their position with the kids and church, and brand new people take their places. The new comers then start over from scratch, seldom being trained or mentored to fill the position from the previous leaders. They may or may not find out about the same books, tapes, videos, and conferences the last group of children's ministers gleaned from. Thus with no guidance, they then only know to do with children what was modeled before them in their lifetimes, i.e. the traditional Sunday School/Bible story mentality they were raised with, which has led us to the current crises. So we find ourselves in a constant revolving door in trying to make substantial, permanent changes in the way we spiritually disciple our children in Christian circles.

For this reason, we need to reach the ears of publishers of children's curriculums, authors of children's books, producers of video and audio materials, television shows, Bible schools, church planters, missionaries, pastors, parents, and anyone else in a position of influence in the body of Christ. More than ever before, if we are to win the battle of transforming our children into spiritual champions, we must link arms and voices to get our message out because we can work our whole lives in our individual fields and not see much more accomplished than what we have right now. But if we work together, we have a better chance of making our voices heard and making a permanent, lasting impact. You need only to do a quick search on the Internet under "Palestinian children" to see how serious our enemy is about training their kids to walk in their vision. At all costs, we must redefine children's ministry in the 21st century if we are to save this next generation spiritually.

Becky Fischer

Part One:
The Need

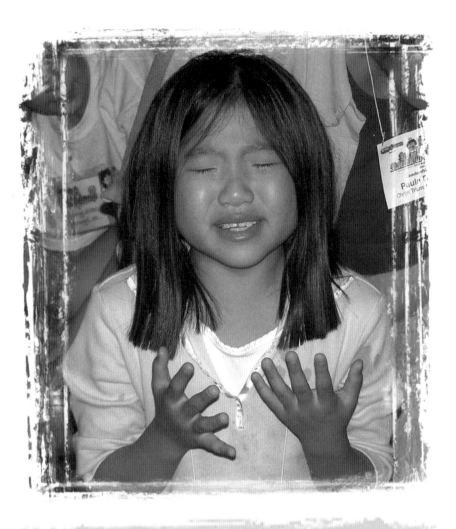

Kids are hungry for reality church and Christianity. They want to REALLY feel His presence. They want to REALLY hear His voice. They want to REALLY experience His Power.

Kids Need to Experience God

"I Hate Sunday School—It's So Boring!"

I was quietly sitting in my front yard one evening reading a book, when I heard a slight commotion at the end of the block. My house was the middle of three on our street, and I looked up just in time to see a blonde-headed girl about eleven years old giggling, cutting across the neighbor's lawn, and heading straight for me. I had no idea who she was. Without warning she ran behind my chair, dropped to her knees, and crouched down so she couldn't be seen. She continued to giggle while telling me, "We're playing cops and robbers and I'm a robber. If my friends catch me, they'll put me in jail."

I cheerfully played along with her, acting as her lookout while her friends one by one appeared at the corner gazing all around in search of their 'thief.' They disappeared momentarily as I gave her a play-by-play report of what they were doing. She hadn't been next to me for more than three or four minutes, when suddenly after a brief pause in conversation she blurted out, "I went to Sunday School today, and I hate it! It is so boring!"

I was a little stunned by this total stranger wondering where such a comment came from in the midst of our game of cops and robbers. Yet it was painfully honest and obviously on her mind. I felt like the Holy Spirit had set me up for the encounter confirming something I had believed for quite awhile. It was that a significant number of kids feel exactly the same way she did about the Sunday school programs they attend.

Cautiously, I asked her which church she went to, and she named one of the larger Charismatic fellowships in our town. I knew the place, however I was only somewhat familiar with its children's program. But the truth was, she could have named just about any of the churches in our city, and with very few exceptions her statement could have been made about any one of them. Why? Because Sunday School and children's ministry as it is typically presented today really is spiritually "boring" even though we have better programs, better curriculums, better technology, bigger budgets, and is more entertaining than we've ever known in the church world. Yet something is still missing.

Sunday School Emphasis Day

Not long after the incident with my young neighbor girl, I received a phone call from a pastor's wife in another part of the state. She began by saying a gentleman in charge of their children's program had asked her to invite me to be the guest speaker for a "Sunday School Emphasis Day." They wanted to impress upon the children of their church how important attending Sunday School was.

"Don't tell me—let me guess," I interrupted. "You're having a hard time getting your kids to come to Sunday School on a regular basis."

> Why are we not able to significantly impact our own children and keep them as active members of the body of Christ after having the opportunity to influence them throughout their most impressionable years? We obviously are not doing much "impressing."

"Right!" she admitted, and told me about how discouraged their worker was. "We're hoping if we have a special day to let the kids know how important it is, it will motivate them to come more regularly."

"I can certainly come and help you," I responded. "However, I'm not sure it will do any good. I can bring in all my exciting sermons and object lessons, and we can have a great move of God. I can tell them how important it is for them to go to church. But what happens after I leave? Your workers will go right back to their same old ways the kids consider boring."

I wasn't trying to be rude. This was simply an effort to make a serious point. The truth is a large number of churches often find themselves in similar situations. Why is this? I truly believe churches are doing their best to provide what they feel is what the children need and want in the way of ministry. Many Bible schools now have courses in children's ministry and some even offer degrees in this area to train people for working with children. Across the nation there are a number of superb conferences whereby children's ministers can get on-going equipping and training resulting in having some of the best qualified children's ministers the world has ever known.

In decades past too often Christian products of any kind were inferior to what the world produced, but that has dramatically changed. We now have some of the highest quality videos, music tapes, CDs, DVDs, books, and some of the most creative curricula and vacation Bible school programs we've ever had in the history of Christianity. But no matter how much better our programs are by virtue of all our improvements, most churches are still missing the point. It's not about building a "better mousetrap," of facilities, curriculums, equipment, better teachers, paid full-time staff, or holding Sunday School Emphasis Days. These are wonderful and we're grateful to have them, but we must search deeper for a solution in order to reverse these problems.

What is the Real Problem?

It's disturbing enough to learn many children view Sunday School as boring after all our hard work. But the real tragedy is what happens as a result of this. Recent surveys from The Barna Group reveal once children reach thirteen to seventeen years of age the numbers who continue attending church dwindle dramatically, and an alarmingly small number of young people "take Jesus with them" after high school. One survey estimates that less than one out of three teenagers plans on continuing to attend church after they leave home.[1] That's almost 70% of the children we have raised.   This has frightening implications for the future of our churches, as well as the state of Christianity as a viable influence on our culture, not to mention what will happen in the lives of these young people without an ongoing Christian influence. Those of us who have been a part of the church world for a good length of time didn't need the surveys to tell us this. We've watched it happen for years. The survey simply put some hard data into what we already knew and experienced— that of watching a mass exodus of teenagers from the church.

They're Not Impressed

While church growth by new converts seems to be expanding rapidly in other continents such as Africa, South America, and Asia, just the opposite is true in the West, particularly America. If this is true, the least we should be able to do is hang on to our own offspring and keep them in the "fold." We have to ask ourselves why we are not able to significantly impact our own children and keep them as active members of the body of Christ after having the opportunity to influence them throughout their most impressionable years. We obviously are not doing much "impressing."

> We must ask which is more important—for our kids to know how many stones David picked up to kill Goliath, or to know the voice of the Master in their everyday lives?

I distinctly remember the days when Catholics proudly proclaimed, "Give us a child until he is seven years old and we will have him for life!"[2] What did they know that we don't know?

Other results from The Barna Group has shown two out of three children still do not know Jesus as savior by age thirteen, that most of them do not know what worship is, and only three out of ten are absolutely committed to Christianity.[3] I can add to these thoughts from my experiences as I travel around the world and the United States and ask for a show of hands in churches almost everywhere I go. Only a fraction of our children are filled with the Holy Spirit, speak in tongues, have ever heard the voice of God, know what it is to be led by His Spirit, or are aware of feeling His presence in a church service or otherwise. In other words, regardless of denominational affiliation, they have no legitimate, working, intimate relationship the Living God on any level after twelve years of being under our tutelage. What's wrong with this picture? We must ask which is more important—for our kids to know how many stones David picked up to kill Goliath with, or to know the voice of the Master in their everyday lives?

Changes Needed in Youth Ministry

An article in *Ministries Today Magazine* by Barry St. Clair, founder and president of Reach Out Youth Solutions, stated about teens, "Youth ministry as an experiment has failed. Much of our effort is like plowing concrete. We plow with the latest techniques and technology. We create a lot of sparks and noise along the way. Then we look back with bewilderment at the lack of harvest. If we want the church to survive, we need to rethink youth ministry. As the late youth ministry expert, Mike Yaconelli suggested, for young people to have a faith that will last, we have to completely change the way we do youth ministry in America." [5]

Though these comments were made specifically about teen ministry, follow them through to their logical conclusion. You have to realize the failure did not begin when these churchians became teenagers. Consider the fact that it's in the first five years of life the foundations of a child's belief system are established, and everything he learns from then on is filtered through this belief system.[6] Author Esther Ilnisky says, "that whatever attitudes and associations our children develop early on regarding church, church leaders, and, ultimately, God, will stay with them for a lifetime."[7]

Children Are Not Seriously Discipled

One of the most grievous errors we believers have made is assuming children are not capable of understanding or acting on the deep things of God's word. Consequently they are never seriously educated or discipled in Christianity, but are merely pacified for twelve years with entertaining little Bible stories via the latest technology. We have mistakenly assumed this was the only way we could hold their attention. The very earliest we have felt they are able to function intelligently and deeply as believers or begin making a difference in the world as Christians is in their teens.

The church as a whole has highly underestimated the spiritual potential of its children because they have primarily seen them after the flesh and not after the Spirit. It's been most difficult to visualize squirmy, wiggly, smelly, sticky-fingered children as prophets and prayer warriors while they are still children. Certainly we can see potential of what they will be "when they grow up." But as children? That's a different matter. We need to get a revelation that if we wait until they are adults to take them seriously as disciples of Christ, it's too late.

> If we have not totally captured the hearts of our children by the time they are ten, eleven, and twelve-years-old, it's possible we will completely lose them when they reach their teen years.

Making Christ Relevant to Kids

It's apparent that church as we know it, Christianity as we live it, and God as we have portrayed Him seem to be quite irrelevant to many in this generation as they mature into their teens and beyond. Jesus, in many ways, is in the same category as Santa Claus, the Easter Bunny, and the tooth fairy to them because He's seldom made real in their lives. Their opinions are largely formed by what we have presented to them on a weekly basis in our Sunday Schools. In many instances, Jesus is just the man in the stories, and not someone they relate to in every day life. Why? Because they've never felt His presence, heard His voice, or seen a real miracle or healing. In too many cases they've seen too few answered prayers, and what is Christianity all about anyway—good Bible stories or a personal relationship with the living God?

If we have not totally captured the hearts of our children by the time they are ten, eleven, and twelve-years-old, it's possible we will completely lose them when they become teenagers. We cannot blame the tumultuous teen years. The problem begins way back in children's ministries that have no life and no sustaining power to undergird these kids as they grow up, no matter how professional and entertaining they are.

What Goes Wrong?

These youngsters may continue to attend church for awhile because a parent forces them, but they make a decision as early as the ten or eleven years old that church is not for them. Use my neighbor girl playing cops and robbers in my yard as an example. As I've since watched her go into her early teen years, she wants very little to do with church. She didn't make that decision after she reached middle school or junior high. Her decision was made long ago when she was the most reachable and found Sunday School boring. What is it in our children's programs that goes wrong? Every publisher of church curricula has gone to great lengths to upgrade and improve their materials and bring them current with present day teaching styles.

Perhaps this is will give us a clue. One of the big reasons people have for not wanting to commit to children's ministry of any type is, "I'd help, but I don't want to miss out on the move of God going on in the adult services!" Or how about the one that normally comes from the head pastor to his children's pastor: "Make sure you organize your schedule so you can sit in the adult service at least once a month. After all, you need to be fed."

Revealing Statements

These are fascinating and very revealing statements about the state of our Sunday School and children's church programs. We are admitting first, there is no presence or move of God in them, and secondly there's no spiritual feeding taking place. Creating a type of spiritual environment where the children are actually able to experience God rather than just learn about Him is imperative to changing children's attitudes towards church. If we as adults crave the presence of the Holy Spirit, doesn't it make sense our children hunger for Him as well?

> Creating a type of spiritual environment where the children are actually able to experience God rather than just learn about Him is imperative to changing children's attitudes towards church.

Reality TV vs. Reality Christianity

Adults don't like attending spiritually dry, dull services. Once they discover there's an alternative, in most cases, you can never get them back to their old churches. Children are no different. They want to experience the reality of God as well. Kids hunger for an encounter with the Holy Spirit, although they don't necessarily know how to verbalize it in this way to us. "Dry and dull" actually have very little to do with whether one has the trappings of the latest technology and the newest and greatest teaching materials. It has to do with no presence of Jesus Christ in the classroom. We can have a bare room and not a stitch of equipment or materials, and have profound services if we will learn to take children into the throne room of God. Too often, we as church leaders have confused using the latest and greatest technological tools in our services thinking this is what a child would consider spiritually stimulating. There is nothing wrong with using every tool available to us to make our services the best they can be. I use many of these in my own ministry. But there is no substitute for the presence of the Holy Spirit.

We hear a lot about "reality TV" these days. Reality TV is a type of television programming filmed live and unrehearsed with real people as opposed to paid actors. They are willing to compete with others doing bizarre, daring, risky, and many times obnoxious things in order to win a significant prize. It may be a huge sum of money, a potential mate, a high paying, prestigious job, etc. Because the prize is so attractive, they are willing to try anything to win. In reality TV you see every step of their journey as it actually happens, and it can be very thrilling, and captivating because the viewers know it's real versus actors who have been paid to put on a good make believe performance. The audience can relate to what's happening because it is real.

Kids Hunger for a Real God

Kids are hungry for reality church and Christianity. They want the real thing. They want to *really* feel His presence. They want to *really* hear His voice. They want to *really* experience His power. If we're honest, these things very seldom occur in the average weekly children's service in churches today. If they don't experience Him inside our children's ministries, where will they go to find it, and how can they ever be spiritually satisfied without it? Occasionally our church camps are places where children can truly experience a move of God. But a once a year experience is not going to sustain them in their Christian walks any more than it can sustain adults.

As church leaders we find it very difficult many times to recruit and maintain a good team of children's teachers and ministers. Could this be one of the reasons? If we are not feeling the presence of God in our children's services, we don't want to be there. We consider it a waste of our time. So why do we think the children will feel any different?

Being Culturally Relevant

As someone has so aptly said, "Our message never changes, but our methods must be culturally relevant." It's wonderful to now have such quality Christian resource materials at our disposal that are in every way competitive with what the world produces. But just being able to use flashy DVD music videos and PowerPoint presentations isn't all there is to being culturally relevant. This is a generation that thinks differently than the generations before them. Contrasted with our high tech environment, we now live in a society that is chasing down every type of spiritual and mystic experience they can find from New Age, to eastern religions, to Satanism.

Because of the loosening of the immigration laws, our nation is the most religiously diverse on the planet. This is no longer an environment where we can assume every child has the same Judeo-Christian background and frame of reference we were raised with in the 20th century. To them truth is relative. It has resulted in a generation that thinks nothing of mixing a little Christianity with a tish of Buddhism, a tad of Islam, and a dash of Wicca. They see no conflict in this because to this generation, power and faith are based on what one experiences, not necessarily correct doctrine. In other words, if someone has a profound spiritual experience through an eastern religion, it's the experience that validates the religion, regardless of whether or not there's any underlying truth in its doctrine.

> Spiritual hunger and awareness are on the rise in our culture, and children are as affected as everyone else. We must bring them authentic experiences in God's presence.

Harry Potter More Real Than Jesus?

To put it even more bluntly, if a child messes around with Harry Potter and experiences something spiritual, whether good or bad, it becomes much more real and valid to him than a Sunday School class in which no power of any kind is ever felt. Kids are hungry for the supernatural, and unless they are taught, they have no discernment of which type supernatural is good and safe and which is not. Anything supernatural is real to them. They simply chase the supernatural like a moth attracted to light. One look in our school libraries, the comic book section of the local grocery stores, and the kids section at Barnes & Nobles will shout about their hunger for ghosts, goblins, witchcraft, and other strains of the occult, which is all a part of the dark side of the supernatural. Spiritual hunger and awareness are on the rise in our culture, and children are as affected as everyone else. We must bring them authentic experiences in God's presence. The logical place for this to happen is in the local church.

Kids Need Their Own Experiences With God

Not long ago I received a newsletter from a very well-known Christian leader who is also a bestselling author. He's been a significant figure in the body of Christ for many years and you no doubt would recognize him if I named him. He is now a grandfather. His entire newsletter was lamenting his concern over his grandchildren, most of who were born again and in some cases Spirit-filled. His concern was over the lack of spiritual interest and hunger he saw in those children as they were growing up in the church. Though their parents were serving the Lord, and their churches were strong, the children seemed to be unaffected by it all. After a lengthy analysis, he finally concluded the reason was that they had never had their own significant, personal experiences with our supernatural God for themselves.

This is so typical. Why aren't our children experiencing something significant in the Holy Spirit on a regular basis? They come to our churches every Sunday for years. We adults are having our own encounters, and hungrily seek after more. It's possible the church this man pastors could be lifeless, but I doubt it. I would speculate the adults of his church would tell you they feel the presence of the Lord on a regular basis.

My first question would be what is their children's ministry like? Is the presence of God tangible on a regular basis? Or are twelve year olds still being fed a steady diet of Moses crossing the Red Sea, Jonah and the whale, and the fruits of the Spirit in much the same way they were when they were four years old? Have they ever been taught about the Glory of God, been taken into the Holy of Holies through worship, learned about the power of the blood of Jesus, and been taught how to hear the voice of the Shepherd? Do they know by personal experience that He's real and not just for people over twenty-one?

In Conclusion

Churchianity has some strange ideas of what our kids can handle and enjoy spiritually. Our children are victims of being trapped in an old wineskin of our preconceived ideas of what they are capable of experiencing as spiritual beings. Being loaded with the latest technological trappings is only one part of being culturally relevant. Regardless of the format of our children's services, Sunday school, children's church, or any other, we must make every effort to see that God is tangibly present in every children's service. We do this by setting apart times of genuine worship where we consciously make them aware of God's presence, taking them into His very throne room. It comes as we make time to sit quietly in our services listening for His voice and sharing what we hear and see with each other. It happens when we provide times at an old-fashioned altar where kids are encouraged to take time to seek His face. As we lead by our personal example, they will follow. By doing so, we will take the first major step in redefining children's ministry in the 21st century.

Taking Action

1.   How do you think the children in your ministry feel about it? Would they tell you it's exciting or boring, and why?

_____

_____

_____

2.   If you have been in your church for five years or longer, make two lists of young people high school age or older who were raised in your church. Make one list of those who no longer attend church, and another of those who still do even if they live in a different community. Which list is bigger?

_____

_____

_____

3.   List ways you currently create opportunities in your children's services for the kids to experience God in some way.

_____

_____

_____

We can either let the world teach our kids how to save baby whales, or we can teach them how to save souls. The choice is ours!

What to Teach Children and Why

Repackaging Noah's Ark Again

My father was a pastor, so I was one of those children who cut their teeth on the proverbial church pew. I had been in church all my life. I loved it, and loved the Lord. We were blessed to have one of the best children's ministers of the day in our church. But at about twelve years of age I distinctly remember sitting in one of our kid's services thinking, "If I hear the story of David and Goliath one more time I'm going to scream!"

My spirit was hungry for more of God, and I knew I was capable of more mature subject matter than what was being given in our children's services. It was frustrating being told the same Bible stories over and over I had been hearing from the time I was a preschooler. Yet this still goes on today in churches all over the world. No doubt this is one of the contributing factors that turn older children off, especially for those raised all their lives in the church. This certainly leads to spiritual boredom and ultimately concluding the church has nothing of significance to offer them. According to Barna's Research, once again the average thirteen-year-old has the attitude that he knows everything there is to know about Christianity, and therefore has no interest in continuing church attendance or learning any more about God.[1] Could this be the result of the constant repetition of the basic Bibles stories throughout their lives? How long would we as adults survive on such a spiritual diet? What makes us think our kids can survive on it?

Some publishers of Sunday School materials have recognized this, and have switched to teaching on moral, relational, and social types of issues the older children can relate to, trying to address what they are encountering in their lives as they mature. This is not all bad, since we in the church should be the ones setting the standard on these subjects. There is definitely a place for this in our children's spiritual education. However, it still misses the major point of what's really missing in our children's ministries, and what children are really hungry for, which is a true encounter with the Living God.

His Ways vs. His Acts

We leaders in the church world at large have been excellent at telling our children about the "ACTS of God." But we've been terrible about teaching them "His WAYS!" **He made known his ways unto Moses, his acts unto the children of Israel** (Psalms 103:7 KJV). It is in knowing His ways we are able to interact with the Lord of Glory. Telling children the acts of God includes telling them all the wonderful Bible stories such as Samson and Delilah, the walls of Jericho tumbling down,

> What children are really hungry for is a true encounter with the Living God. They must be taught how they can become daily participants in His glory and power.

Peter Walking on Water, Lots wife turning to a pillar of salt, and so on. In them the children can clearly see what God did and is capable of doing again, i.e. His actions.

But in teaching them His ways, we equip them for their own personal life of answered prayers and signs and wonders. The ways of God are learned as we enter into prayer, worship, hearing His Voice, being led by His Spirit, entering into the baptism in the Holy Spirit, healing the sick, understanding and flowing in the Gifts of the Spirit, and more. We make a grave mistake if we do not believe children can learn the ways of God, i.e. why and how He does what He does in our lives. But to teach them these things we have to rethink the types of topics and subject matter we present to them on a regular basis.

Unending Parades of Bible Stories

The church world in general from parents to pastors, children's ministers to the writers of children's books and materials have a very limited list of what they think kids are capable of understanding, and what they are interested in. Go into any Christian bookstore on the planet (which is merely reflective of what the public is demanding) and check out the children's section. You will find an unending parade of the basic Bible stories redone a dozen different ways, from books, coloring pages, videos, dramatized audiocassettes and CDs.

You will find material on the Fruits of the Spirit, the Armor of God, the Ten Commandments, obedience to parents, topics like fear, sharing, and other character building issues, Christmas, Easter, and why we don't do Halloween. Numerous times I have walked through these stores shaking my head and wondering, "Just how many ways can you repackage Noah's Ark anyway?" As good and necessary as these subjects are, we are still missing the point if it is the only thing we present to our children. Although they are a vital part of our children's spiritual foundations, these things by themselves are not enough to feed our children long term. Kids are desperately hungry for a touch in their spirits from our incredible Creator! They must be taught how they can interact with the Most High God and become daily participants in His glory and power.

We've been on the right track by telling them about the miracles of Jesus, but we've not taken it to the next step by explaining to them what they can do to see similar miracles in their own lives. This is going to require some rethinking about what and how we teach them.

What is Milk and What is Meat?

We frequently talk about the "milk" of the Word versus the "meat." Often someone will comment about a sermon they heard calling it "meaty," meaning it was intellectually challenging and stimulating, bringing out deep truths from the Bible. "Milk" on the other hand is the basic, most commonly known concepts and doctrines of the Scriptures.

We know from the natural world that milk is for infants and babies, primarily because they have no teeth to chew with and their stomachs are not ready to digest complicated food items. On the other hand, a thick beefsteak is suitable for adults because they have both strong teeth and a more highly developed digestive track. The same holds true in the spirit. There are truths that go down easily into our spirits, and others we have to "chew on" for awhile to get the full meaning. When a person is newly converted, we call them a babe in Christ. We begin discipling them by feeding them on the simplest, most basic truths of God's Word, i.e. is the milk. As they grow in the Lord and are able to comprehend and handle deeper concepts, we begin to feed them on the "meat" of the gospel.

Conventional thinking in regards to children is that as long as a person is a child they can only handle the "milk" of the word. We have designated milk to include what we listed earlier in this chapter, such as the basic

> Conventional thinking in regards to children is that as long as a person is a child they can only handle the "milk" of the word. This is an idea that has to be seriously challenged.

Bible stories, the Ten Commandments, fruits of the Spirit, etc. This is an idea that has to be seriously challenged as we begin redefining children's ministry in the 21st century. If you think it through logically, even in the natural, it is only the newborn infants and toddlers that continue to drink their mother's milk. Even if they continue to breast feed longer, they still begin taking in solid food at around five months. It is only in early infancy and babyhood they exist solely on milk alone.

Why then have we decided that spiritually our children can only handle a diet of spiritual milk until they are twelve years old? Especially children who are raised in the church, and have committed Christian parents, can begin eating the meat of the Word at very young ages. They may not be able to eat an entire twelve ounce steak like adults can, but they can take lots of small pieces off that big steak—maybe two to four ounces—and eat it just fine. They've got the teeth, and their stomachs can handle it. The only difference is the size of the portions they can hold.

Hungry Kids in Hogansville

A church in the tiny town of Hogansville, GA invited me to do a week long series of children's services some years ago. They told me their little church had gone through some difficult times and they had lost a number of families. As a result they said they only had about seventeen children attending their services on a regular basis. So in preparing for the services, this is what I pictured and planned for. I was assuming I would be speaking to their group of children who had been raised in the church all their lives.

Our topic was going to be on the Blood of Jesus, one of my favorite subjects from the time of my own childhood. I carefully gathered my object lessons and visuals, which included a small gold painted Ark of the Covenant and my High Priest costume for studying the Old Testament temple sacrifices. There was also my cat-of-nine-tails, a big cross, a goblet of fake blood and other items to explain how the shed blood of Jesus paid for the healing of our bodies, plus more. All of my lessons were actually quite deep for children, and were atypical of what you normally teach youngsters.

Not Your Average Church Kids

When my team and I arrived in Hogansville, we found out the church family had gone to great lengths to comb the small city and gather up as many children as they could. One couple had a van in which they were bringing in loads of kids from some of the low-income areas well known for drugs, homosexuality, crime, violence, neglect, and every problem that goes along with them. They were obviously not your average church kids raised on Moses in the bull rushes.

In hearing this I became very concerned that my lessons were going to be way over their heads, and wondered what I was going to do. They were expecting at least a hundred kids each night with only seventeen of them being their own. But I was too far away from home to go back and put a new set of lessons together. There were no options for me but to go ahead with what I had prepared.

We threw our hearts into the services and from the very first night the children were incredibly receptive. When we gave the call for salvation, most of the visitors raised their hands to receive Jesus. As is my custom, each night before starting the next lesson, I gave review questions to see what they'd learned and how well I had taught them. They were sharp as tacks answering the questions perfectly even using church and scripture terminology they had heard the night before which we knew was not familiar to them.

> We keep kids on pabulum and milk for twelve years then wonder why they can't wait to abandon ship the first chance they get.

We saw these children dramatically touched by God's presence, hearing His voice, seeing little visions, and experiencing profound healings in their bodies. At the end of the week, the pastor's wife came to me saying, "I've been in ministry with my husband for fifty years, and have worked with the children much of that time. I never knew till now that you could teach children such deep things."

What's sad is she is typical of most of the church world. Our children are spiritually anemic for lack of real spiritual food and in redefining children's ministry in the 21st century, we as parents, pastors, publishers, and children's ministers must radically rethink the things we are teaching our children. We keep them on pabulum and milk for twelve years, and wonder why they can't wait to abandon ship the first chance they get. It's better for our children to know God, than to merely know all about Him.

To actually know Him, requires a different strategy and teaching topics than we are presently using in our children's ministries.

What Are Kids Capable of?

We are living in a day when average children in the secular world are doing outrageously phenomenal things. Whether it is accomplishments in school, science, music, or sports, children are setting records in ways we could never have imagined even twenty-five years ago. It's amazing to discover teens as young as fourteen and fifteen years old are Olympic stars. How early did they have to start training to reach those goals? Many of them begin when they are as young as four and five years of age.

It's unbelievable to learn that kids and young teenagers are often responsible for the major onslaughts of computer viruses that have crippled the entire nation at one time. Where did they learn so much about computers, when half the adults today can barely figure out how to send an email? Kids are incredibly capable of some very adult concepts and activities.

I like to collect articles and stories about the amazing feats of children. There was one in a national children's magazine which featured a group of kids ranging in age from thirteen to eighteen who were trained fire fighters in their Alaskan community. Their job included emergency rescue work such as saving people who had fallen threw thin ice or were trapped in avalanches. The article said these youngsters, who make up over half of the fire fighters on their squad, wear beepers to school and are regularly called out for emergencies. They take up to four hundred hours of training every year to keep them equipped for the job. They are being trained for life and death experiences—their own and others. Most adults would never dream of placing children in positions of such serious responsibility.

A few years ago the national news media featured a twelve-year-old boy who had begun a ministry to street people. It all started when he was driving with his dad through their city. He asked his dad why people were lying on the street. His dad explained they had no place else to go. It was a cold time of year, and the boy immediately begged his father to take him home, let him remove the blanket from his own bed in order to give it to a man on the streets. He soon began collecting blankets from others and regularly took them to street people until a full-fledged, full-time ministry was birthed from it.

A friend of mine who is also a children's minister, Pete Hohmann, wrote a book entitled *Kids Making a Difference*.[2] It centered on the amazing accomplishments of children in this generation. One story that stands out is about a group of fourth grade children (average age eleven years old) who learned there was still slave trading going on in the African country of Sudan. Their teacher informed them women and children were being bought and sold for as little as $50.

They were first horrified to learn slave-trading was still occurring in our lifetime, but immediately become proactive to address the problem. They wrote to the President, the First Lady, Oprah Winfrey, Bill Cosby, and Steven Spielberg. To make a long story short, as the news media began to pick up the story, these children raised enough money to free 100,000 slaves. By June 2000 due to the efforts of the children, Congress

> The Church is still passing out coloring pages of Adam and Eve and wondering why our own kids are not being captured by our message.

passed the Sudan Peace Act, which placed economic pressure on Sudan to stop the slavery. As of 2004, slavery has nearly been eliminated, all because of the efforts of a group of "tweeners."[3] Most adults would probably never consider bringing such serious subject matter before children. They would feel there would be no point to it and that it would unnecessarily burden children with overwhelming knowledge. They would certainly never expect children to be able to do anything about it.

The World Knows Where to Take Its Message

In my community, when the police want to run a campaign about buckling seat belts in your vehicles, their first strategy is to take their message to our public schools. They teach the children how important it is, then run a contest for the children to draw pictures and posters on it. The winners then have their drawings made into billboards which are erected around the city. For a month or more everywhere we look is artwork of children informing us of the importance of buckling up. The same thing happens when the American Cancer Society wants to run a campaign on the dangers of smoking. Their first line of attack is to go to our children, and again, we see their artwork on billboards everywhere. The world knows the importance of reaching the children first with their very meaty messages. For one thing, they know if they reach the kids, they will keep them as converts for life as well as reach the adults.

Special interests groups know the value of reaching the children with their political agenda. Our schools are flooded with materials teaching kids about saving the rain forests, stopping pollution, ways to keep the ozone layer from deteriorating any further, etc. This generation takes it very seriously and gets involved in a variety of ways. We might wonder if children should be burdened with such adult topics and problems. It can be overwhelming and depressing even for adults at times. But the world seems to think it's okay to pass this information to our kids.

Rethink Our Menu of Topics

The world system is indoctrinating them on about every adult issue you can think of. Yet the Church is still passing out coloring pages of Adam and Eve and wondering why our own kids are not being captured by our message. We must redefine children's ministry in the 21st century to include a passionate, meaty message that compels them to get involved with the gospel. The wonderful and much loved videos of Adventures in Odyssey and Veggie Tales are a tremendous blessing to the children of the body Christ and thank God for them. But they will not take our children into their spiritual destinies! We need to rethink the menu of topics we present to our children. As the body of Christ, we have a decision to make—we can either let the world teach our kids to save baby whales, or we can teach them how to save souls! The choice is ours. This is a generation that will be committed to something. Let's train them to be committed to the Kingdom of God from their earliest days.

We have somehow been content to keep even serious messages to our children on the level of lighthearted entertainment. Enough already! It's time to dim the lights, not to watch another Bible Man video, but to shut ourselves and our kids in with God and soak in His presence to learn to hear His voice and discern what He is saying to this generation!

Charles H. Spurgeon (1834-1892), known as "the Prince of Preachers" and one who is honored across denominational lines as having impacted Christianity forever, had much to say on the subject of children in his sermons. One of his comments was that children are capable of much more than we have given them credit for. He said they are capable of not only evangelizing themselves, but of pastoring themselves as well.[4]

> It's time to dim the lights, not to watch another Bible Man video, but to shut ourselves and our kids in with God, soak in His presence, and discern His voice and what He's saying to this generation.

This is unthinkable to most adults! And yet is that not what street gangs do in the inner cities of the world? They make their own converts and become a guardian family to all who belong, regardless of the fact it is grossly perverted. Street children all over the world experience this very thing.

I'm not saying we should train our kids to start pastoring churches. But I am saying we need to be stretched in our views of the spiritual potential of our kids, which will force us to reconsider our tactics as children's ministers and leaders in teaching, equipping, and discipling them. We must reevaluate everything we've been doing in this regard.

What Should We Be Teaching Them?

It's necessary for us at this point to challenge status quo thinking as to what spiritual milk is. To do this, let's review Hebrews 6:1-3 (NLT) to see what the Bible calls "milk."

"So let's stop going over the basics of Christianity again and again. Let us go on instead and become mature in our understanding. Surely we don't need to start all over again with the importance of turning away from evil deeds and placing our faith in God. You don't need further instruction about baptisms, the laying on of hands, and the resurrection of the dead, and eternal judgment. So God willing, we will move forward to further understanding."

Let's dissect what it's saying here. The basics of Christianity are obviously the milk. According to the writer of Hebrews, the basics include:

1. ***Turning away from evil deeds.*** This would be repentance, salvation, and walking in holiness and righteousness.

2. ***Placing our faith in God.*** Faith is a huge subject covering everything from believing God created the universe, to believing God for the healing of our bodies, provision of our needs in every area of life, finances, signs and wonders, and more. Entire movements in the body of Christ are centered on the topic of faith, so there's obviously a lot to be said on this topic.

3. ***Baptisms.*** This includes seven different baptisms named in the New Testament, but we will concentrate on only three:
   a. Baptism into Christ, or our salvation (1 Corinthians 12:13)
   b. Baptism in the Holy Spirit with power and boldness (Acts 1:8)
   c. Baptism in water, implying commitment (Matthew 28:19)

4. ***Laying on of hands.*** This includes:
   a. Bestowing divine blessing on someone as when Jesus laid His

hands on the children (Matthew 19:15)
b. For newly baptized people (Acts 16:19)
c. Leaders and missionaries consecrated to service
(Acts 6:6, 13:2-3; 1Tim.4:14, 5:22)
d. The Holy Spirit was stirred in people by this act (Deu.34:9;
Acts 8:18-19)
e. Healing the sick (Mat.9:18; Mar.16:15-18; Act.14:3)
f. Some would add a transference of anointings. (2 Timothy 1:6-7)

5. The resurrection of the dead.

This would include Jesus' resurrection, which we must believe to
be saved (Romans 10:9). It also includes the resurrection of
hundreds of saints at the same time as Jesus' resurrection, as well
as Lazarus, Jairus' daughter, and the resurrection of the dead in
(1 Thessalonians 4:16), which includes us. There were also a
number of others as well.

Even kids who are being raised in so-called Christian homes attending our churches on a regular basis can have a surprising mix of other beliefs thrown into their theology.

6. Eternal Judgment.

This would be hell for the unbelievers, and the bottomless pit for
Satan and his cohorts. It would naturally include a study of the
rapture, the second coming of Jesus, heaven, and the Great White
Throne Judgment, and other end times subjects.

There are actually some heavy duty topics in this list. A good share
of them are on the "meat" list in many of our churches. But the Bible
considers them "milk," which means we will have to rethink what we
teach children if we are going to be in sync with the scriptures.

Basic Christian Doctrines

There are a number of other basic Bible doctrines which should be taught to children that are not listed in the Hebrews passage. These include such:

1. Godhead as the Three in One: Father, Son, and Holy Spirit
2. The infallible, inerrancy of Scripture as the Word of God
3. God as the creator of the universe
4. Man created in God's image, spirit, soul, and body
5. The original sin of man
6. The virgin birth of Jesus
7. The deity of Jesus (or Jesus as God)
8. In Incarnate Christ, God taking the form of Man
9. The sinless life of Jesus while on earth
10. The role of the church to spread the gospel
    (aka The Great Commission)
11. The Millennial reign of Christ at the end of the ages
12. New heaven and new earth, where we will forever dwell with
    the Lord

These points may vary slightly from church to church, but are generally accepted in the body of Christ as the fundamental doctrines of Christianity. Through the years there have been some denominational churches who have successfully taught systematic Bible doctrine to their children though it is not widespread throughout Christianity. Unfortunately it is not very common in charismatic circles. One movement even wrote their own curricula to teach all the basic doctrines to their children by the time they were five. It also included training them to minister. This would be a worthy goal of any church choosing to do it.

As we have discussed, there is such a diverse spectrum of beliefs in the world these days, we can no longer assume our church children know all of the things we've just listed. Nor can we assume they have ever even heard them specifically taught, much less believe them. For instance, one of the most shocking results to me that came out of Barna's research in

Real Teens, is that most teenagers no longer believe Jesus lived a sinless life on earth. Nor do they believe the devil is a real entity, but rather a symbol of evil.[5] I'm curious to know how this happened. Did they believe as children, but were talked out of it when challenged in their teen years? Or did they never believe it and if so, why not? If they did believe it at one time, why could they be talked out of it so easily as teenagers? I can't help but to wonder what type of teaching, training, and discipling they received in the local church as children.

Surprising Mix of Beliefs in Christian Homes

Even kids who are being raised in so-called Christian homes attending our churches on a regular basis can have a surprising mix of other beliefs thrown into their theology. Take for example something as simple as the very common present day notion of speaking to the dead, which is now heralded all over TV, periodicals, and books. What does the Bible have to say about this? It's an abomination to God! But do we ever spell it out to our kids in our churches? How will they know if we don't tell them especially

If the kids in Palestine can be taught to kill the Christians and Jews, and if the Wiccans can teach their kids to cast spells on people, then we can teach our kids to cast out demons and raise the dead through the name and power of Jesus.

if their parents or relatives believe in such activity? Though this type of information may not be considered basic Bible doctrine, in our culture it should certainly be included in our teachings somewhere.

Few people, including some Christians, believe Jesus is the one and only way to heaven these days. They believe He is just one of the choices, and it may happen to be their choice, but they basically believe all roads lead to heaven. For the first time in American history our kids are sitting next to Muslims, Hindus, Wiccans, New Agers, Buddhists, and more in their public schools. Today when a group of children have a discussion about "God" they have to clarify "which God" they're talking about.

So as a matter of clarification, among other things we need to be adding to what we should be teaching our kids is once again the foundations of our Christian faith. Even for kids who are in solid homes and know these things, the unfortunate truth is they now live in a world where they will be forced to defend their Christian faith. They need to know what, and more importantly, *Who* they are defending and why.

Heavy Duty Topics

No doubt there will be those who will strongly criticize me for making these next statements, but I defer to the Word of God on this point. Just before Jesus ascended into heaven, He gave the disciples, and us, some last minute instructions to carry on the work He began on earth. It is commonly known as the Great Commission, and is a basic fundamental truth in the Word of God every child should be taught in our churches. In Mark 16:15-18 He said, **"Go into all the world and preach the gospel to every creature."** He continued, **"And these signs will follow those who believe: In My name they will cast out demons; they will speak with new tongues; they will take up serpents; and if they drink anything deadly, it will by no means hurt them; they will lay hands on the sick, and they will recover."**

As I read this, and many other passages, I see no place where Jesus put an age limit, or any other limiting criteria on doing these works, which are known as a part of the believer's ministry. When He said, "Go!" He did not say "all grown-ups go," or "all moms and dads and pastors go." Nor did He say, "Everyone go! But you kids need to wait until you're twenty-one!" He said to every believer, "Go." That means all of us. Whoever names the name of Jesus as Lord and Savior, must go or be guilty of disobedience to the Master.

Likewise, there are no restrictions on the other points as well. He says "they that believe" will have signs following them, such as casting out demons, speaking in new tongues, and laying hands on the sick. We can also add raising the dead. Whatever Jesus did, He said we would also do and even greater things. Jesus said, **"Most assuredly, I say to you, he who believes in Me, the works that I do he will do also; and greater works than these he will do, because I go to My Father"** (John 14:12).

Why not kids? Nothing in that verse puts a restriction on anyone because of gender, race, or age. If a child believes, he or she qualifies to do the works of Jesus just like anybody else.

If the kids in Palestine can be taught to kill the Christians and the Jews, and if the Wiccans can teach their kids to cast spells on people, then we can teach our kids to cast out demons and raise the dead through the name and power of Jesus. That doesn't mean I'm into designing conferences and holding classes for kids on how to cast out devils and raise the dead. But there are some fascinating instances when kids have done these things simply because someone told them it could be done, which we share in a later chapter just for your information.

> We need to set the bar a little higher. We need to get a revelation that our children are far more capable of comprehending and acting on the deep things of God's Word than we've ever considered before.

Miscellaneous But Important

More than ever before our children should be taught not only God's Word and the believer's ministry, but a healthy dose about their Christian heritage. In the same way children are naturally interested in their ancestry, and how "grandpa came over to America on the boat" as he sought religious freedom, they need to know about the rich spiritual ancestry they are a part of as members of the body of Christ. It's extremely important for them to hear about the great heroes of our faith, such as William Tyndale who was burned at the stake because he dared translate the Holy Scriptures into the language of the common people.

This includes men like Gutenburg who dared to print the Bible on printing presses at great personal risk.

Though it may seem extreme, older children and especially teens should be encouraged to read Foxe's Book of Martyrs or D.C. Talks "Jesus Freaks." The sad truth is we can no longer afford to mince words with our kids. They are now living in a day and age where many young people may be required give their lives for the sake of the gospel. Children and young people in other nations are doing it all the time.

Other great Christian books would include *The Cross and the Switchblade* by David Wilkerson, *The Hiding Place* by Corrie Ten Boom, *The Light and the Glory* by Peter Marshall, *The Heavenly Man* by Brother Yun, the amazing stories of Smith Wigglesworth, Billy Graham's life story, and other great books of Christian heroism. Also very valuable reading are the biographies of such tremendous missionaries such as Amy Carmichel, Hudson Taylor, William Carey, John G. Lake, and others who carved out the gospel in some of the darkest places on earth.

Any books on current American sports heroes who are true committed Christians, would also be of great benefit. With the older children, you can use Sunday School or midweek class time reading as a group. Have a contest. For every book they read they earn points towards a worthwhile prize (it doesn't have to be expensive). You can also spend five minutes in each children's service for a "history moment" after the offering, or right before the sermon, where you give short excerpts of the stories of these people. Be creative. But let your kids see how they are connected in history to a much larger body of believers than their own local church.

In Conclusion

All I am suggesting by mentioning these things is we've got to start thinking some new thoughts in regards to the spiritual training of our children if we're going turn things around in our children's ministries and the future of Christianity. Whatever you teach adults can be taught to children if you break the thoughts into small enough pieces, and liberally use visuals and objects in your presentation. In your mind, it may be far too much of a stretch to even remotely entertain the thought of teaching your kids to cast out devils or raise the dead. That's okay. But then let me ask you, what can you reach for? Where can you begin that will take you farther than you're going now? Can you stretch enough to teach them how to hear the voice of God and be led by His Spirit? I challenge you to step into some uncharted territory if you're at all concerned with what's happening now in your children's ministries and want to see things turn around.

Today as Christian ministers and parents we need to seriously reconsider the types of things we are typically teaching our children and why. We need to set the bar a little higher. We need to get a revelation that our children are far more capable of comprehending and acting on the deep things of God's Word than we've ever considered before. Then we need to reconsider the whole concept of what the "milk" of the Word is versus the "meat" of the Word. We need to realize we have a long way to go to teach our kids even what the Bible considers milk. We must understand if we're going to raise spiritually healthy, grounded Christian children, we've got to get off the treadmill of limiting their spiritual diets to the same old Bible stories over and over again, especially as they enter the preteen years. We must learn to feed our kids some spiritual meat, which will sustain them through the most challenging times of their lives. In doing so, we will be redefining children's ministry in the 21st Century.

Taking Action

1. List the topics you have taught your children in the last twelve months. Beside each one write whether you feel it would be classified as "milk" or "meat" based on the discussion in this chapter.

_____

_____

_____

2. Do you have a well-thought out plan as to what topics you want to be teaching your children over the next three years? What topics will you include now that you probably would have never considered before? _____

_____

_____

3. Just for fun, take a trip to your local Christian book store, walk around, and count how many different ways Noah's Ark has been produced in every format from books to figurines. How many and what forms did you find?

_____

_____

_____

Our children's ministries must become clinics of functioning Christianity.

True Discipling & Mentoring of Children

Families that Pray Together

I was on a mission trip in India when I was unable to sleep any longer on the unyielding hard bed. I reached for the TV remote in my hotel room in the early morning to see if I could catch any news from back home. I quickly found an English speaking station just as the camera zoomed in on a modern looking Middle Eastern family. The first words the narrator spoke were, "You've heard it said the family who prays together stays together." "Wonderful!" I mused. "I've stumbled across a Christian program of some sort."

But as I continued to watch, my excitement turned to shocked disbelief while this reporter described the annual ceremony this family was about to participate in as dedicated Shiite Muslims. This mom, dad, and two sons, approximately nine to eleven years old, were in a modern kitchen sharing a meal together. They looked like a very average family. Then before the announcer continued to explain this unusual event that was about to begin, he gave some history behind it. It seems hundreds of years ago Mohammed's grandson went to war with his enemies, and there was no one among his Muslim brethren who were willing or interested in going with him to help. As a result he died in battle as a martyr.

Brutal Penance

Since that time every year the faithful Shiites take one day to do penance—physically brutalizing themselves and shedding their own blood as punishment for not helping this important man in their history in battle. The form this penance takes is that the men, using razors, cut a big slice in the tops of their heads, then literally pound the wound with all their strength forcing it to bleed. They don't just do this once, but repeatedly throughout the entire day.

Dad Leading the Way

Just then the camera focused in on this well-dressed, well-educated father taking his straight edge razor, and with someone's help to part their hair, he whacked his sons on the top of their heads creating gashes in their scalps. I watched stunned as instantly the two boys began to beat themselves on the wounds until blood began to trickle down their faces. Then it wasn't just once, but they continued to beat themselves at the encouragement of their father until their faces and shirts were covered with their own blood, and it had splattered on the lens of the camera.

> It was noteworthy how the father deliberately involved his sons in the very middle of this gruesome event rather than be content to merely tell them about it, or even let them observe from the sidelines.

This family then joined a long procession of their comrades marching through the streets of their city shouting, waving their arms, and beating their heads. As the camera stayed glued to the bloody sight before us, the announcer explained it would be the busiest day of the year for the ambulances. The men often became seriously ill and faint due to the energy they were exerting, while at the same time losing enormous amounts of blood. Some of the men in the march were literally drenched from head to toe in scarlet red. The story concluded as we watched the young boys and their father sitting at the end of the day, understandably fatigued, and quiet. The father shared he had participated in this march for the first time when he was only three years old, but that he had waited to start his sons until they were seven. Though they all admitted to being frightened the first time they participated, it was now just a part of life.

Committed to the Cause for Life

This horrendous event hung with me for days. As I reflected on it, two thoughts occurred to me: 1) those boys will never be neutral about their faith, and 2) short of a miracle of God, they will never leave their faith. The kind of involvement and commitment they have been mentored into will be imbedded in them spirit, soul, and body for life.

It was noteworthy how the father deliberately involved his sons in the very middle of this gruesome event rather than be content to merely tell them about it, or even let them observe from the sidelines. Instead he took the time to personally take part in their spiritual education, giving new meaning to the term "discipling."

Also impressive was that he involved his two young sons—just little boys—in a very adult activity. He himself was initiated into this ceremony at the ripe old age of three by his own father. One might surely wonder why a preschooler was forced into such a grotesque ritual, but this man's dad obviously did not want to waste any time immersing his son "in the faith." No wonder by the time Muslim youngsters reach their teen and college age years they are ready to die for what they believe in.

Line Upon Line, Precept Upon Precept

Someone has said, "You teach adults, but you train children." Their reasoning was adults already have a foundation of skills and tools for doing and thinking the way they do. But children don't have the same point of references and have to be taught to do things from scratch.

Anyone who works with kids regularly realizes it's not enough to verbally tell a child to make his bed, brush his teeth, or feed the dog if he's never done it before. It's necessary to actually demonstrate how these things are done, then allow them to do it by walking them through on a step by step process. Most of the time they need to be shown repeatedly before they can do it well. That's training. Teaching, on the other hand, is just giving someone verbal information and instructions.

The story of the Shiite Muslim father and his sons should give us an entirely new perspective on the type of spiritual discipling we as parents and churches should take towards even the youngest of the children in our care. Deuteronomy 6 gives us great insight into the prescribed way for parents to raise their children:

> *4* " Hear, O Israel! The LORD is our God, the LORD is one! *5* "You shall love the LORD your God with all your heart and with all your soul and with all your might. *6* "These words, which I am commanding you today, shall be on your heart. *7* "You shall teach them diligently to your sons and shall talk of them when you sit in your house and when you walk by the way and when you lie down and when you rise up. *8* "You shall bind them as a sign on your hand and they shall be as frontals on your forehead. *9* "You shall write them on the doorposts of your house and on your gates.

> It's not enough to tell children they can hear God's voice. They need to be trained what to hear and shown how to listen. It's not enough to tell them Jesus can heal the sick. They need to be shown how to lay hands on the sick themselves.

How can we know how young we should begin to train our children in the ways of the Lord? Isaiah 28:9-10 has the answer:

> "Whom will he teach knowledge? And whom will he make to understand the message? Those just weaned from milk? Those just drawn from the breasts? *10* For precept must be upon precept, precept upon precept, Line upon line, line upon line, Here a little, there a little."

More than Just Another Buzz Word

It's not enough to tell children they can hear God's voice. They need to be trained what to hear and shown how to listen. It's not enough to tell them Jesus can heal the sick, and they can too. They need to be shown how to lay hands on the sick by watching you do it, then doing it themselves. This is what Jesus did when he trained his disciples.

We come up with a lot of different buzzwords in the body of Christ that are sort of the "hot topic" of the day. In the past some of the buzzwords have been "faith," "prosperity," "revival," "seeker sensitive," "the prophetic," and so on. One of the current buzzwords as of the writing of this book is "discipling." It seems every church these days is actively "discipling" people in their congregations. But if you listen closely enough, you discover all in the world they're doing is holding one more Bible study during the week. To me that's not discipling.

Mine may be a narrow viewpoint, but my definition of discipling is doing what Jesus did. He walked, talked, and lived life with His disciples, showing them how to teach, preach, heal the sick, open the eyes of the blind, cast out devils, and pray, then he sent them out to do the same things on their own. He was there when they had their successes (**"Master, even the demons are subject to us in your name!" Luke 10:17**) and he was there in their failures (**"Oh, faithless generation.... This kind only comes out by prayer and fasting!" Mark 9:29**)

Jesus Walked Them Through the Process

But He walked them through the process after they had watched his example over an over again, no doubt up close so they could see every miraculous detail the rest of the crowd couldn't see. That's discipling. Disciples followed Jesus where he went, watched what He did, and then they imitated Him. That's how we disciple children.

We can't go live with the children in our ministries, nor can we bring them home to live with us. So in a more modern setting we must take advantage of the time that we do have together in our weekly children's services and model, demonstrate, and train our kids to do the works of

Jesus. This includes prayer, worship, hearing God's voice, being led by the Spirit, operating in the gifts of the Spirit, healing the sick, doing prophetic ministry, and more. We not only explain to them what it is, but we show them what to do then help them do it. A wonderful children's minister by the name of John Tasch uses this formula to disciple children:

1. I do—you watch
2. I do—you help
3. You do—I help
4. You do—I watch.

That's discipling. That's training. That's what you do with children.

> We must abandon the more traditional, less effective mentality of "I preach—you listen" to "Come on up here and let me show you how to do this."

Effective Teaching Methods

In the midst of our discussion of redefining children's ministry in the 21st century, we must abandon the more traditional, less effective mentality of "I preach—you listen" to "Come on up here and let me show you how to do this." Even in the public schools the most effective teachers now try to recreate different environments in their classrooms to enable the students to actually become participants in the learning process.

For instance, instead of the traditional methods of teaching math with addition, subtraction, division, etc. on paper or chalkboard, they will create a business center in the room, and every child has to build a "store" or a business. As they conduct business out of their little store, they do math problems that are related to the real world while dealing with their "customers" and "vendors." The effectiveness on the learning process is profoundly greater than simply sitting and cracking out math problems on a piece of paper, although that may still be a part of the process at some point.

In the American school system two excellent examples of discipling children would be "Shop" and "Home Economics" classes. In shop classes boys, and sometimes girls, learn things like carpentry and how to build everything from coffee tables and bird houses to real houses under the guidance of their teacher and coach. In home economics, girls and sometimes boys, learn to sew clothing, cook, and other domestic tasks. In both courses children learn very practical, beneficial skills that will help them their entire lives. Their skills are learned not through reading books or even listening to lectures, but by a hands-on approach where they actually do the work. For at least an entire school year, these kids cook, sew, and build things everyday they're in class. They learn by doing.

These are the very same things we as children's ministers must learn to do in order to make active participants in the Kingdom of God out of our children—making true disciples that know how to walk out their Christianity in their homes and schools. Whether we're teaching children why they close their eyes and raise their hands when they worship, to teaching them how to speak to sickness and disease and command it to leave a person's body, our children's ministries must become clinics of functioning Christianity. It's when children become active participants in Kingdom activities that their Christianity becomes practical and beneficial in their everyday lives.

Teaching What No One Has Taught Me

I was speaking in a children's ministers conference in Dar Es Salem, Tanzania on the importance of teaching children how to hear the voice of God. I had stressed it several times over the days I was with them. Finally between workshops, a young woman quietly asked to speak to me, and with tears in her eyes she asked, "Please, Mamma Becky, will you teach me how to hear the voice of God? No one has ever taught me. How can I teach the children if no one teaches me first?"

Her request was sincere and is far too common among children's ministers, and even Christians as a whole, not just about hearing the voice of God, but also about healing the sick or operating in the gifts of the Holy Spirit, etc. It's a legitimate problem. How can we teach something no one has ever taught us? I run into this dilemma regularly as I train children's workers in local churches.

I've Never Been the Same

I grew up in a Pentecostal denomination that believed in healing the sick and even had it included in their basic tenets of faith. And yet we seldom actually saw anyone get "divinely" healed, which usually meant an instantaneous or otherwise miraculous, unexplainable healing. Still we faithfully clung to the belief all our lives. It wasn't until Charles and Frances Hunter came through our area with one of their Schools of Healing that

> Nobody told me you couldn't teach children these "adult" activities. We immediately began to see and hear of healing miracles.

I saw and experienced my first healings. The Hunters never touched one of us. They taught us what to do then had us turn to the people standing around us, and we prayed for the sick. The first time I ever experienced having someone being slain in the Spirit when I laid hands on them occurred in those meetings. For the first time in my life I prayed for someone, and they were instantly healed. I also needed healing, and a friend prayed for me, and I was instantly healed. Those experiences changed my life. Someone taught me what to do, showed me how it was done, then released me to do it. I've never been the same.

It just so happened at the time that I was "taking my turn" in children's ministry in my home church, as all good church members did. I didn't know any better than to begin teaching the children in our Sunday morning service exactly what the Hunters had taught me. Nobody told me you couldn't teach children these "adult" activities. We immediately began to see and hear of healing miracles. To this day when I go back for a visit, there are parents who will say, "I'll never forget when you taught our kids how to pray for the sick. Our whole family was down with the flu, and they prayed for us, and we all got healed!" But it came because someone not only taught me, but showed me what to do, and released me to do it.

You Can Learn

If you find yourself in this situation of being willing to train children but have not been trained yourself, let me encourage you to try several things. Depending on the area of ministry you wish to train kids in, go to your pastor, tell him/her what you're doing, and ask them if they would be willing to take the time to train and mentor you in the specific area you're interested in. Hopefully, they will jump at the chance, or if their time is at a premium and can't do it themselves, they will at least tell you who else in your congregation might be able to help you.

In addition to this, remember that the Holy Spirit is your Teacher. With His guidance find as many good books, tapes, or videos on the subject and begin to train yourself. You can learn whatever you want to by applying a little bit of effort to find resources and others to help. Pay close attention to how Jesus did things in the Bible, such as in the area of healing. Then being led by the Spirit, practice on every sick person you can find, even if you make a lot of mistakes, or don't see very many results. Hunters told us, "If you pray for a thousand people and you never see any of them get healed, don't quit praying because eventually it will happen. Then your faith will increase and so will your successes." You need to take the same advice. If you have the money, go to healing conferences where you know they will be specifically training the people to do the ministry.

If you're interested in learning how to hear the voice of God, or operate prophetically, find some conferences where they will be training and releasing the people in attendance what to do. Whatever area you feel you need help in, just know that God will honor your efforts. If you are never able to get to those types of conferences, and you can't afford the books and tapes, begin praying that God will send people across your path that can help you learn what you need to do. Then boldly step out and use what knowledge you already have. These areas are all things He desperately wants you to know how to do, so He will lead you along the way. Even the Benny Hinns of this world had to start somewhere. They did what they knew to do, and God increased their understanding and knowledge as time went on. Over time they became more successful.

> If it is true the body of Christ needs to be equipped for the work of the ministry, children should be at the top of the list of potential trainees because they are so teachable and open to new ideas.

Kids should be exposed to as many areas of ministry as possible so by the time they're adults they know exactly what they're called to do and will be experienced at it. I've seen documentaries where doctors said they knew by the time they were ten-years-old they wanted to go into medicine. I heard an interview with Olympic star Carl Lewis who said at age five, he was already jumping the cracks in the sidewalk practicing to make his dream come true to become a gold medal winner in track and field. Even my weatherman on a local TV station said he knew when he was only eight or nine years old what he wanted to be a when he grew up! Called "His Holiness," the 14th Dali Lama of Tibet, 69-year-old Tensin Gyatso was crowned as spiritual leader at only five years of age. I've been told leaders of the Islamic religion often select little boys as young as two and three years old and mentor them all their days in the Islamic faith. Our enemies seem to be miles ahead of us in this area. No wonder their young people are so insanely committed to their cause. It's been bred into them since they were old enough to walk!

If it is true the body of Christ needs to be equipped for the work of the ministry, children should be at the top of the list of potential trainees because they are so teachable and open to new ideas. If the world knows the value of mentoring such little ones, where should we be at as the body of Christ?

It's More than Ministry Of Helps

In recent years there has been some excellent teaching for children's ministers to encourage them to allow children to be involved in every facet of their services. This includes using children on puppet teams, drama teams, running sound equipment, running video cameras, being ushers, teacher helpers, and so on. We heartily endorse using children everywhere possible. They are very capable, willing workers and should be trained early in all areas of ministry of helps.

But we want to encourage you not to be content to limit your children to these natural areas of practical helps. That's all fine and good, but there are only so many slots to plug kids into, and there's so much more to serving God than these things. Not only that, but they can get lulled into thinking those areas are the only ministry they're capable of or should be interested in. That's the problem we have with adults right now. People are trained to be ushers but not to give life-changing prophetic words over the people who daily come across their paths. Christianity is supposed to be a life-style. It's something that is to be taken outside the four walls of the church. Outside of helping in special outreaches, puppetry, drama, running cameras and sound systems is not something they will use in everyday life. More importantly, as wonderful as it is to teach them these skills, they aren't going to change lives or equip them to be participants in the works of Jesus. We are to teach our children to become ministers of light and life, not merely to be puppeteers.

By all means, continue to use them in these areas. But don't stop there! Go on to disciple your kids to do the works of Jesus. Train them to be evangelists, prayer warriors, intercessors, worshipers, healers of the sick, those who hear God's voice and follow His leading, and so much more. It's supposed to be everyday Christianity. Don't ever let it be said of the children under our care, "They never felt the presence of God nor ever heard Him speak to them." If that happens, we have failed in our responsibilities to truly disciple our children.

> Don't ever let it be said of the children under our care, "They never felt the presence of God nor ever heard Him speak to them." If that happens, we have failed in our responsibility to truly disciple our children.

In Conclusion

As children's ministers and parents we must begin to adjust our thinking about training kids to include active, deliberate, on-purpose, hands-on mentoring. This must include showing our children how to do the work of the ministry of Jesus, not just telling them about it, and then releasing them into it by giving them regular opportunities in our weekly children's services and other places. We must realize they are capable of doing everything Jesus did, and that He put no limits on who could or couldn't do signs, wonders, and miracles. As the caretakers of the children we must take discipling and equipping to a new level, and in doing so we will be greatly helping to redefine children's ministry and thus Christianity in the 21st century.

Taking Action

1. Describe how you have been mentoring your kids in some area of spiritual ministry.

_____

_____

_____

2. What are some ways you could modify your weekly services to include hands-on training in some area such as prayer or evangelism, etc.?

_____

_____

_____

3. Make a list of people in your church you might be able to recruit to help in mentoring kids in areas of ministry.

_____

_____

_____

It should be just as common to hear that a church has a children's prayer team, a children's healing team, a children's prophetic ministry team, and a children's evangelism team as it is to hear they have a Sunday School.

Determining Our Purpose

The History of Sunday School

Sunday School began in the general era of the infamous tale of Oliver Twist written by Charles Dickens. It was the days of the little match stick girls and chimney sweep boys in England where families were so poor they were forced to engage their children in various forms of labor to help meet their financial needs. Many of those children spent their entire lives in factories. Because they were compelled to work, they were not able to get an education of any kind. Therefore, generation after generation grew up never learning to read or write. This created a cycle of poverty for without a decent education they were never able to do anything but menial jobs. Crime and corruption were constant themes in these young lives, and finally one dedicated Christian man by the name of Robert Raikes (1736-1811) decided something had to be done to stop this pathetic merry-go-round of poverty.

He determined to teach these young street urchins to read and write by holding an informal school. He recruited as many lay people as he could to help with this huge project. The plan was to gather up the children on the only day of the week in which they did not have to work—Sunday. They sat them down at desks, gave them paper and pencil, and one textbook—the Bible—and began to teach. Thus Sunday School was born. The year was 1780, and by 1831, Sunday School in Great Britain was reaching as many as 1,250,000 children weekly which was about 25% of the population. For many children it was the only education they ever received. Sunday School has been called the "greatest lay movement since

Pentecost." It was certainly responsible for it's own type of "revival" in that day.

We must wholeheartedly applaud and bless the place Sunday School has had in the history of the world. There is no doubt many lives were changed because of it touching every area of life and culture of the times! Thank God for Robert Raikes and all the nameless helpers who dedicated themselves to this great work. They not only helped these children in very practical, tangible ways, but also laid a solid biblical foundation in their lives which undoubtedly affected all of society.

It was only after Raikes and his companions blazed this unique trail that the churches in England began to take note of the good it was doing. They decided they too would hold "Sunday School" under their own church programs, although not as reading and writing education, but primarily as Bible education.

> Could it be that what we have been perpetuating for generations in children's ministry as a whole is a two hundred year old wineskin that today is producing limited results?

For the most part, what we call Sunday School today has changed very little since those days. Many traditional Sunday School programs still sit the children down at tables and chairs in much the same fashion as public school. They are given papers, which are textbooks (sometimes called 'quarterlies' or workbooks) and pencils to write with. Of course, the Bible is the basis of education as it should be. The children are separated according to age groups as in regular school systems. The atmosphere is normally quite similar to a typical school environment.

External Changes Aren't the Issue

Later an alternative to the actual Sunday School format was developed.

It was the children's worship service. A children's worship service, otherwise known as children's church, though more prevalent now, is still not as popular as the Sunday School format. It is structured after an adult worship service with its own praise and worship time, sermon, and offering.

In a children's church style service it is not necessary to divide the children into various age groups. Instead, kids ages six to twelve years old can all meet together as a group in one room. This eliminates the need for a lot of separate classrooms and so many teachers to fill the positions. In more recent years, cell groups have been developed for kids as the cell church concept has grown worldwide. But the spiritual ho-hums can be prevalent in any of these styles of ministry if the presence of God is not evident in the meetings.

Occasionally there have been life-changing ministries that rise to the surface such as Child Evangelism Fellowship or the Sidewalk Sunday School movement. What makes these and others like them so successful and powerful is that they are consumed with a vision to change lives. But aside from the handful of organizations such as these, it is interesting to note that on the whole, there have been very few creative new thoughts in children's ministry over the years.

I'm not referring to things like the addition of external trappings such as games, contest, puppets, drama, or balloon sculpturing into to our methodology. It has nothing to do with colorfully decorating our rooms and painting animals and angels on our walls to make things more visually attractive. It's not even about creating curriculum utilizing a hands-on approach through the five physical senses. All of these things certainly enhance the learning experience, and we should be using everything we can to make a child's church experience fun and exciting. But what I'm talking about has to do with core philosophies of what it is we're called to do in raising children as followers of Christ.

A Two Hundred Year Old Wineskin

In spite of everything we have just mentioned, could it be that what we have been perpetuating for generations in children's ministry is actually a two hundred year old wineskin that today is producing limited results?

On the one hand, the fact Sunday School is still being used speaks highly of the original God-breathed idea. On the other hand it could be a symptom of the prevailing thought that children are not capable of handling anything more than basic Bible stories, snacks, and coloring pages, so why change things? It could also be reflective of mindsets like, "Well, it was good enough for grandma, so it's good enough for us too." Or lastly, it may be folks have viewed it and thought, "If it's not broken, don't fix it." But if Barna's research is accurate, and we are in fact losing our kids by the droves when they grow up, then we have to consider the possibility that something about our system is broken, and desperately needs fixing.

> If we can be truthful with ourselves, there are thousands of churches doing Sunday School purely because it's what everybody does or it's what's expected of them, and not because they burn with a vision.

Again, structure and format are not the problem. The reality of Jesus can be felt mightily in any setting if there is leadership who knows how to bring the presence of the Lord in. Bottom line is, we need to examine why we're doing what we do, and what our goals should be. In planning a children's ministry in our churches, whatever structure or format we take, or external trappings we use, we need to ask ourselves **"What is it we are trying to accomplish in our children's ministries?"**

Without a Vision the People Perish

People such as Robert Raikes are visionaries who receive powerful ideas from God and run with them. As they become successful, others come along and see the success, so they copy the original idea. There's nothing wrong with this as long as they are following the leading of the

Holy Spirit in doing so. That's the whole key.

But if we can be truthful with ourselves, there are thousands of churches doing Sunday School purely because it's what everybody does or it's what's expected of them. It's not because they burn with a vision for children, or have received direction from God. Churches realize something needs to be done for children, so they just do what everyone else is doing with little thought behind what we are trying to accomplish or what their goals should be. They assume it will be successful in their church because it's been successful in other churches—or so it seems.

Perishing Collectively

What happens as a result is we end up with a lifeless program that becomes a continual problem. With no real vision, leadership to run it becomes an issue. We all know the scripture that says, "**where there is no vision, the people perish**" (Proverbs 29:18). This is one of those places it could be argued where we're perishing collectively!

Nobody wants to be a part of something that carries little to no anointing, or where it seems teachers are just baby-sitting kids, so it becomes hard to find willing workers to lead the classes. No one would dare use this terminology, but truthfully too often children's ministry in a local church is seen as a "necessary evil" and not really an important part of the whole vision of the local church. But this might possibly stem back to the same mindset that children are not really capable of very much spiritually anyway, so the best you can do with them is entertain them in a back room somewhere so the parents can get ministered to. Hopefully this book is crushing that outdated mentality once and for all. But where do we go from there? **We need to start with a vision.**

What's Our Purpose as Children's Ministers?

In seeking God for a vision for the children in our homes and our congregations, there are two questions we should ask ourselves:
1. "What does a child who is a committed "follower of Jesus" look like?"

2. "What will it take to get him/her to that level?"

We may each have varying opinions on these two questions. However, the Bible can help give us some clues as to what the answers might be. First it tells us, we are to love the Lord with all our hearts, minds, and souls, and love our neighbors as ourselves—that is be sincere, devoted worshipers. Secondly, we are to be lovers of the Word of God and people of prayer, having a personal regular interaction with the Lord. Third, we are to be filled with His Spirit walking in might and power. Fourth, as His sheep we are to know His voice and follow His leading, and fifth we should be imitators of Jesus in everything we say and do. This will speak to character issues and integrity of the heart. Six, we are to be about our Father's business. This includes doing everything He's called us to do from spreading the good news of Jesus in any way we can, to healing the sick, opening the eyes of the blind, ministering to the brokenhearted, setting captives free, casting out devils, and raising the dead, and so on.

> I dare say, it seldom occurs to most adults that children need to be equipped for ministry at all, and in most cases, it never occurs to a children's minister that this is a part of his/her responsibility. But it truly is.

A Flock Within a Flock

As children's ministers, we're in an interesting position. We have been set over a flock within a flock. The head pastor, who is presumably a fivefold ministry gift, has been placed in his body scripturally to "equip the saints for the work of the ministry" (Hebrews 4:11). That's one of his primary jobs. But he has placed us over the shepherding of the children, which means in essence we are responsible for equipping the "little saints." I would dare say, it seldom occurs to most adults that children need to be equipped for ministry at all, and in most cases, it never occurs to a children's minister that this is a part of his/her responsibility. But it truly is, and if we don't do it, it's not going to get done. If this is the case, it sheds some very specific light on what our purpose and vision should be in the local church.

It should give us clear direction on the types of things we should be teaching and preaching to our students, and help shape what our children's ministries will look like in the local church. Everything we do and say in our limited period of time with our kids should be shaped by this purpose. Remember, among other things, we're the spiritual foundation layers in the lives of our children. And the foundation we lay, good or bad, is all they are going to have to build on for the rest of their lives in many cases.

Fresh Ideas To Consider

As a short review of what we have discussed thus far in this book, we want to remind ourselves where we're going with these next concepts.

1. Kids are hungry for a genuine encounter with the Living God. Therefore, we want to provide them with a variety of ways to experience this.
2. We want to raise the standard on the topics we have typically taught our children, and begin to bring in some real meat for them to chew on.
3. We want to keep in mind children need more than another sermon. They need the hands-on opportunity to get up and actually do what they're being taught, applying it to their lives in a very personal way.

This all leads us to the next step. We need to actually do some equipping. It should be just as common to hear that a church has a children's prayer team, a children's worship team, a children's healing team, a children's prophetic ministry team, and a children's evangelism team as it is to hear they have a Sunday School. In these, and other areas such as prophetic arts, missions, and more, children will experience the reality of God's presence. They will be taught the meaty things of God's word, and they become active participants in the work of the ministry. This changes everything for the children. Boredom and disinterest become nearly a thing of the past. I can tell you from first hand experience if you begin to involve your children in these types of things, they will never be the same again! There will always be some children you are never able to break through due to many issues in the home, etc. but as a whole, this will dramatically impact your children.

The following ideas are not original with me. There have been a number of children's ministers using them for years, but in quiet, hidden, out of the way places. Very few people have really noticed them. What I am proposing here, is that these types of things need to become **mainstream children's ministry**. In addition to impacting the children, consider what it might do in the overall ministry as far as your teachers and helpers are concerned.

> Boredom and disinterest become nearly a thing of the past. I can tell you from first hand experience if you begin to involve your children in these things, they will never be the same again!

Square Pegs in Round Holes

We all have met those volunteer teachers who have totally struggled to study the Sunday School quarterly on Saturday night, completely frustrated because it just doesn't flow easily for them. But they do it because they said they would, and they like you and want to help. They really don't mind working with kids, but this Sunday School class thing is just not for them. They feel very much like the proverbial square peg being pounded into a round hole. Let's name one of them "Mrs. Anderson." Let's say Mrs. Anderson does not really enjoy teaching nine year olds. Where she really shines, however, is in intercessory prayer.

Why not take her out of her frustration of teaching a traditional

Sunday School class, and ask her instead to lead a children's intercessory prayer team? Rather than restrict the age group, allow any children in your ministry to sign up. Ask her to do it for at least three to six months, then reevaluate at that time whether she wants to continue. Certainly there is more than one person in your church that loves to pray. Perhaps one loves to pray for the nations, while another loves to pray for the pastor and the families in the church. They could each mentor different small groups in prayer giving each small group of children genuine one on one mentoring and equipping in what is normally considered an adult activity. You accomplish many things at once. You still get the extra worker you need, but you create excitement, enthusiasm in both teacher and students and create an incredible mentoring and learning experience for the children.

What about old "Bob" who is extremely prophetic and easily hears and sees things from God? He's practically an expert in visions and dream interpretation. Even your pastor goes to him for advice occasionally. Why not ask "Bob" to mentor a group of kids in the prophetic? Don't try to stick a curriculum in his hands. Give him the freedom to teach the way he feels led if it makes him more comfortable. He could teach and mentor a small class on Wednesday nights for a couple of months with just a handful of kids, or teach on the subject once a month to your whole group in your Sunday children's church. Whichever way he does it, both he and your children will be profoundly stretched and strengthened. Encourage him to prophesy over the children regularly, speaking destiny, vision, and calling into their lives. Then ask him to train the children to hear and see from God and speak out what they are experiencing. Now you have an excited children's worker because he's working in an area he loves, and is not simply filling a hole in your volunteer staff.

Giving the Term 'Discipling' a New Meaning

Out of this type of discipling, there are all types of possibilities. With the help of others who are gifted in evangelism, you can take a carload of kids trained in the prophetic to the local mall for an hour during your midweek service. Their job for the night is to get words from the Lord for strangers passing by. As they bravely speak those things out to the strangers, hopefully it can lead to opportunities to talk to people about Christ. This is "reality" Christianity.

You may have someone in your church who walks in a great mercy gift and is always visiting shut-ins at the local nursing home, or even works in a soup kitchen for street people. Would he or she be willing to mentor children by going with them and teaching them to pray with and for the people? They can train the children to ask the Lord to give them ideas of how to make a homemade card with a scripture in it that the Lord gave them just for a specific individual. Learning to minister to the widowed and lonely is definitely reality Christianity.

> They will begin to sense the power and presence of the Holy Spirit, and see signs and wonders, and flow in the supernatural. It will begin to satisfy the hunger they have in their hearts to connect to the living God!

What about the individual in your church who really seems to have an anointing in the area of praying for the sick? Would they be willing to train a small group of kids on an regular basis how to heal the sick, teaching them everything they can think of from anointing them with oil to the laying on of hands? They could take them along to the hospital's children's ward to practice what they have learned. It would be "on-the-job" training for your kids to encounter hands-on experience in healing the sick.

As you can see, this doesn't eliminate your regular children's services. In them, you as the leader would lay the groundwork for the others by the sermon topics you preach on. You will be preparing the kids' hearts for getting involved and excited about hooking up in these areas of ministry. These are more like "extracurricular activities." It's still important to minister to the whole group regularly by laying solid biblical foundations, but for those who are hungry for more, there are options, which can profoundly affect them for the rest of their lives. Hopefully these ideas will cause some "lights" to go on in your head about options in bringing children into a real encounter with God and—as the old saying goes—start to think outside the box!

The Possibilities Are Endless

As your children become proficient in their areas of ministry, there will be opportunities for them to work together with adult prayer teams, or adult healing teams. Perhaps your pastor will even provide opportunities occasionally for your children to pray for the sick at the end of one of his/her services, and so on.

The possibilities are endless of what can be done. You may want to have special services where you invite visitors into your services for the purpose of allowing the children to "practice" ministering prophetically over adults. We do this on a regular basis during our summer camps, and in other places, and we are consistently amazed at the level of accuracy children receive words from God. There have been some profound things that we have even captured on video just to show people "what it looks like" when children prophesy and give "words" from the Holy Spirit of edification, comfort, and exhortation (1 Corinthians 14:3).

You may want to organize outreaches in your neighborhood where the children are given the opportunity to pray for people for healing etc. You may even want to organize a missions trip to an Indian reservation or an inner city outreach in your state where they will have the opportunity to use all of their training from intercession, to the gifts of the Spirit, to healing the sick, and more. You are limited only by time, money, and the leading of the Holy Spirit.

These things will radically change the texture and quality of ministry your children receive, and you will dramatically drop the numbers of kids who are bored and become potential church dropouts. They will begin to sense the power and presence of the Holy Spirit, and see signs and wonders, and flow in the supernatural. It will begin to satisfy the hunger they have in their hearts to connect to the living God!

Learning By Doing

I read an interesting book on learning to teach effectively in other cultures than your own. It was written by an American to fellow Westerners about how they must learn to think differently and teach differently in non-western cultures if they wanted to be successful. They gave examples of some top-notch teachers from western nations who went to various obscure people groups and tried to educate native children in the same style of Greco-Roman classroom setting they were accustomed to. In

> If we want to teach in such a way to have the most results and cause them to love learning about spiritual things, then observing and doing is critical.

those environments, they were absolute failures. So they began to observe the cultures they were in. They began watching how the parents trained their children in everything from cooking to hunting, to making clothing, and everything else in their life-styles. They noticed it was done entirely by modeling and mentoring. The author wrote:

"Among the Eskimo, children assume responsibilities early in life and are included in adult affairs. They learn by doing and observing, and adults constantly admonish and direct...

"...The first time I saw my two-year-old daughter with a huge machete in her hand I cringed, but because other children also wielded these sharp instruments, I tried to refrain from reacting like an hysterical American mother by grabbing it. Because knives are an essential part of Yap life, employed to cut brush, open coconuts, and even clean fingernails, parents guide children early in the proper ways to use them."[1]

Our point here is that, much like obscure people groups, children are a culture all their own. They think differently, learn differently, and their values are different from ours as adults. If we are going to become better Christian educators [more accurately—mentors, coaches, and trainers] with the little ones placed in our care, we are going to have to learn how to teach effectively in their "culture." The above example really is exactly the way children should be trained in every society, not only in natural issues, but in spiritual matters as well. It is actually the biblical model given to Jewish families.

There's a lot more to effective teaching than whether or not we use puppets and DVDs in our ministries. If we want to teach in such a way to have the most results and cause them to love learning about spiritual things, then observing and doing is critical. One huge purpose of childhood is to be a dress rehearsal for adult life. We've heard it said, some children learn by hearing. Some learn by seeing. But I can say from my own experience, every child I've ever met learned best by doing!

In Conclusion

I was a business owner for many years running a commercial sign shop. We used computerized methods of cutting vinyl lettering and graphics to make our signs. When people would come to apply for jobs, we'd ask them if they knew how to use computers, and many times the answer was no. We needed people who at least knew the basics, because we just didn't have time to train them in from ground zero.

As we turned them away, they would always add, "But I know I could do it if somebody would just show me how!" We need to remember when working with children that they are spiritually capable of doing everything Jesus did if somebody will just show them how! One of our primary purposes as children's ministers is to equip our kids to get up and out of the pews and do the works of Jesus inside and outside the four walls of the church.

We need to get a fresh vision of what it is we are called to do. We need to ask ourselves what a child who is a committed follower of Jesus looks like, and what it will take to get him/her there. We need to become true equippers of the little saints in the wide world of the ministry. We must lay spiritual foundations, which will make them into active participants in the kingdom of God, and provide them ample and regular opportunities to exercise their gifts. We need to reconsider what mainstream children's ministry should look like. In doing so, we will be doing much to redefine children's ministry in the 21st century!

We need to remember when working with children that they are spiritually capable of doing everything Jesus did if somebody will just show them how!

Taking Action

1. *What are you trying to accomplish in your children's ministry? In other words, what is your vision?*

_____

_____

_____

2. *In your opinion what does a child who is a committed follower of Jesus look like?*

_____

_____

_____

3. *What is it going to take in teaching, training, and equipping to get your children to look like your idea of followers of Jesus?*

_____

_____

_____

Could there have been anyone else other than Eli who could have trained Samuel the way he needed to be trained to carry out the purposes of God on earth? Why did it need to be the high priest? Wasn't there any other priest in the temple who could have done the job?

Eli! Eli! I'm Calling You to Children's Ministry!

The Way It Might Have Been

Eli, the elderly high priest of Israel, lay on his sleeping mat, snoring deeply. Nearby lay Samuel, a child left to Eli's care by a woman so hopeless of ever bearing children for her own pleasure that she had asked to bear one for God's. Her wish had been granted, and she had appeared some time ago to Eli and left him with the young charge to be raised in the temple. It had been an uncomfortable surprise for the old man, but she reminded Eli that he had agreed with and even prophesied the answer to her prayer. Now in the middle of the night the boy and the man lay sleeping.

Thus begins one story of God's answer to a needy nation—a desperate woman offers her womb for God's glory, and a loving God grants her the desire. A special child was born to be raised as a deliverer and judge for a nation that had lost contact with Him. It seems all the players in this drama were alive to the poignancy of a pivotal time in history and in their own lives, except for one drawn in without realizing his significance. Could Eli have remotely foreseen the implications for his own life when he said to Hannah, "**Go in peace: and the God of Israel grant thee thy petition that thou hast asked of him**" (1 Samuel 1:17 KJV)? Through creative license let's go into this drama as it *might* have been played out:

Eli's sleep was suddenly broken as he heard a voice calling, "Eli, Eli!" Groggily, he turned and looked at the little boy, Samuel. The child was not moving but there was no one else in the room.

"Samuel!" he called. No response came. He rose and shook the boy's shoulder. "Samuel, do you need something?"

"Huh? I was asleep, Eli."

"Didn't you call me?"

"No."

"You sure you don't need something? Water? Do you have an ear ache again?"

"No, I'm fine."

Puzzled, Eli lay back down and returned to sleep. The voice came again. "Eli! Eli!"

"Whaaat?" Eli looked around once more and saw no one. He shook Samuel.

"What do you want?" he asked again.

Samuel looked blankly at him. "I'm fine. Really."

"I heard you call me."

"Did it sound like my voice?" Eli's eyes widened a little bit.

"No."

"I really was asleep."

"OK, son. Sorry. Go back to sleep."

Eli walked slowly back to his mat pondering the possibility that was dawning on his heart. Could God be talking to him? He lay down and punched the bolster under his head. It was hard to go back to sleep but eventually he drifted into a half-doze.

The voice came again. "Eli, Eli!"

Head darting up, eyes wide open, Eli replied, "Speak, Lord. Thy servant heareth!"

"Eli," the voice continued. "I have sent you the child, Samuel. He was born for Me to fulfill My need to bring My people back to me. You are to train him and impart to him all that I have given you. He is your chief ministry, your hope for lasting fruit. I will teach you how to minister to children, how to bring him into the things of God. He will be great and your life will be fulfilled in seeing him enjoy the power and success you have longed to see in your own life."

Stunned by what he heard, Eli looked upward toward the spot the voice seemed to emanate from. He lowered himself once again to his mat. For a while he lay there with eyes open pondering what he had heard. Finally, he shook his head and snorted quietly. With a brushing motion over his shoulder, he snuggled back under his covers. "Must have been something I ate," he mumbled. "I *know* God is not calling me to children's ministry!"

Oh, Eli…[1]

Who Is Actually Called to Children's Ministry Anyway?

This story was playfully manipulated by a good friend of mine and was a great source of amusement for us as we discussed the implications. But Pamela's interpretation actually fuels a great deal of serious thought about who really is called to children's ministry anyway. Eli would certainly have been categorized as a "fivefold minister" according to Ephesians 4:11 had he been alive in our lifetime. I cannot help but smile at the thought of the squirming that would take place by head pastors and full-time ministers all over the world at the very suggestion they might called to children's ministry. Yet in quickly looking at the scriptures there are only two examples of individuals that specifically had children's ministries. They were Eli and Jesus Himself—both bonified fivefold ministers, if it's proper to use this modern term with them.

The only other reference to such a possibility was also a leading Christian minister, Peter. It was after Jesus' resurrection in his famous last conversation with Peter that He asked three times, "Do you love me?" As Peter responded, Jesus gave instructions: 1) feed my lambs, 2) tend my sheep, 3) and feed my sheep (John 21:15-17)

Jesus Had Kids on His Mind a Lot

Most of my life I actually made an assumption He was referring to new converts in this passage when He spoke about lambs, because surely He wasn't telling the great Peter he should be ministering to the children—was He? (Even I have been guilty of overlooking children at times!) But I personally do not believe it was a coincidence when Jesus told Peter, another fivefold minister, to feed the lambs. In studying the gospels closely, it is very evident Jesus had the children on His mind a lot. We know He had to rebuke the disciples for their attitudes concerning children at least once. I fully believe this scripture was in fact talking about children, and I don't believe it was coincidence that they were mentioned first, not second or even last the way they might be treated in many churches today. Children have always been an important priority to Jesus. He groaned in Matthew 23:37 (NLB):

> Are we actually suggesting head pastors and other fivefold ministers are called to minister to children? Right now, at this point of crises in the church, everything has to be up for discussion!

"Oh Jerusalem, Jerusalem, the city that kills the prophets and stones God's messengers! How often I have wanted to gather your children together as a hen protects her chicks beneath her wings, but you wouldn't let me."

Jesus' unfulfilled desire in the earth today is still to gather the children to Himself. I've often wondered why Jesus wanted to gather the children, and what He would have done with them once they were gathered. As we look back at our opening story, I find myself asking if there could have been anyone else other than Eli who could have trained Samuel the way he needed to be trained to carry out the purposes of God on earth. Why did it need to be the high priest? Wasn't there any other priest in the temple who could have done the job?

Remember, we're attempting to discuss outdated wineskins, and trying to discern what the Spirit of the Lord is saying to the body of Christ today concerning ministry to children for the sake of the future of the Church. Right now, at this point of crisis everything needs to be up for discussion! There can be no sacred cows in regards to our children. So the question looms before us: Are we actually suggesting head pastors and other fivefold ministers are called to minister to children?

The Fivefold Ministry

In Ephesians 4:11 we're told, **"And He Himself gave some to be apostles, some prophets, some evangelists, and some pastors and teachers, for the equipping of the saints for the work of ministry, for the edifying of the body of Christ."**

Although the term itself does not appear in scripture, these five different types of ministers have come to be known as the "fivefold ministry gifts" among Christians worldwide. For a season, their significance had been lost in the church world, but in the last century, one by one, their uniqueness and purpose has once again been restored to body of Christ. The scripture seems to be clear—in order to fully equip the saints to do what God has called the Church to do, she needs the fivefold ministry gifts to teach, train, and disciple her. This seems to be the primary role of these types of ministers.

In other words, every believer is supposed to be healing the sick, preaching the good news, mending the brokenhearted, setting the captives free, etc., not just the professional clergy. But the majority of us would not know how to do any of it if someone didn't take the time to teach us. That's the role of the fivefold ministry. It is their God-given responsibility to train us to do kingdom business. They are gifts to the body who are called to be coaches, instructors, and equippers in much the same way a coach works with a professional sports team training and equipping them to go on to victory in their games.

A Breaker Anointing

There is something about the apostle, prophet, teacher, evangelist, and pastor that can take us to higher heights and catapult us to new levels of spirituality because of the unique gifts they bring to the local congregation. They have what some have called a "breaker anointing"—the God-given ability to take us further in the Spirit than we can go without them. Many of us can report how things shifted in our lives after sitting under a powerful teacher of the Word. We've been changed as a prophet spoke into us our destinies in Christ. We've rested in the strength and security of a genuine pastor who carefully watches over us in our times of need. We've watched the evangelist move the hearts of sinners no one else could even touch.

The question becomes, "Would not these same kinds of impacts be made on our children if they were directly exposed to these types of ministers, at least on a more regular basis?" It could be argued that God has placed parents in the lives of children to protect, guide, and speak into their lives. True. But is it the same? I believe you could find parents who have been all of these things to their children still tell you that in the presence of a true fivefold ministry gift, there have been significant changes in their children they themselves were not able to make.

Parents have been given a place of importance in the lives of their children that no one else can fill. At the same time, God has placed fivefold ministers in the body to do what no parent, spouse, friend, or other leader can do. And if children are legitimate members of the body of Christ, they need the steadying presence and exposure to mature fivefold ministers in their lives.

> If children are legitimate members of the body of Christ, they need the steadying presence and exposure to mature fivefold ministers in their lives.

It might be argued that purely because they are members of a local congregation with a pastor who is fivefold at the head, this would satisfy the need. Perhaps. But we need only to review the present crisis in the children's ministries of our churches to surmise something in this plan isn't working.

The Steadying Influence of a Spiritual Dad

Not long ago I hosted a four day "School of Healing for Kids" at a church in Missouri. The couple who pastors the church are dear friends of mine. One of the reasons I work with them as closely as I can is the sincere interest and involvement they both make as head pastors in their children's ministries. At this unique children's equipping conference, both Pastor Alan and Pastor Carol sat through all of our teaching sessions with the children. One of my guest speakers leaned over and whispered to me incredulously, "Can you believe the head pastor is sitting in on these sessions? Have you **ever** seen a head pastor sit in on children's meetings?" To which I had to reply "No," with very few exceptions.

Indeed, it is rare to see a head pastor take much interest in the children's ministries of his church beyond wanting to know the needs of the children are being met. In all fairness, they are extremely busy people with many demands on them. They want to know there are quality people in charge of the children's programs, and that everything is running smoothly. I do believe the majority of head pastors genuinely care about the children in their church, but the culture of Christianity and its leadership is frequently one of keeping distance between themselves and the children. It's why they hire children's pastors and Christian education directors. Children's ministers everywhere will testify it is rare to ever see a head pastor darken the door of the children's ministry, and maybe there's nothing wrong with this.

I realize the bigger the church becomes, the more difficult it may be for the head pastor to be personally involved in every area. I am merely suggesting there might be a link to the lack of involvement from the head fivefold minister in the congregation and the lack of spiritual maturity and strength of their children and youth.

Emotionally Absent Fathers

What the Lord showed me as I watched Pastor Alan's involvement particularly (since it is much more common to see pastors' wives involved) was a comparison to the homes where there is a father physically present, but in which he is what psychologists call "emotionally absent." These are homes where even though the children see their hard-working, responsible, moral, father in the house, he seems uninterested or uninvolved in their lives. The children are left emotionally abandoned, uncovered, and left to themselves to evaluate their worth and self-esteem. These kids are usually an emotional mess.

We all have heard enough to know the impact of a dad in the home is huge! I believe it is fair to say it's the same in a church family. Where a head pastor, who is the spiritual father, is involved, engaged mentally and emotionally in the children of his church, they are far more spiritually healthy, on fire, and secure in who they are in Christ than in churches where this is not so. I'm talking about more here than a friendly pat on the head, an occasional hug, and sharing a joke after the Sunday morning service with some of the children who run by.

The Lord says that a man turning his heart to his children is the key ingredient in avoiding the Lord's curse and walking in his blessing. Is it possible God is putting his Holy Ghost spotlight in this area of the church world for it's leaders to consider?

Turning the Hearts of the Spiritual Fathers

What caused me to relate this to Pastor Alan's involvement was the incredible spiritual maturity I have seen in the kids in his church from the preschoolers on up. We could hardly believe it when we found out, among other things, Pastor Alan actually goes into the children's services and preaches to his kids three or four times a year. But it shows tremendously in the spiritual strength of his children.

In the natural, we gain our sense of who we are, where we are going, and our place in the world from our father. The value our father attaches to us gets deeply imprinted on our self-perception. God is in the business of turning the hearts of the fathers to their children and, in turn, the hearts of the children to their fathers (Malachi 4:6; Luke 1:17). In the

Bible, the "heart" indicates the core of a person, i.e. the vital center from which all else springs, the seat of the affections and that which gives focus to a person's life.

It is a remarkable thing the Lord says that a man's turning his heart to his children is the key ingredient in avoiding the Lord's curse and walking in his blessing. Is it possible God is putting His Holy Ghost spotlight in this area of the church world for it's leaders to consider? Our children need fivefold head pastors as spiritual fathers to take interest, be involved, pray over them, prophesy over them, and speak into their lives, individually, and collectively as a group! This doesn't mean they have to take over the children's services and be the regular Sunday morning speaker. But there needs to be some type of meaningful interaction between the spiritual leader of the house with even "the least of these."

Well-Known Ministers Target Youth

But this involves more than just the head pastor of a church. It should also include traveling ministers who walk in the mantle of fivefold authority. It is wonderful to see these ministers laying hands on the children in prayer lines, prophesying over them, and speaking into their lives. This is incredibly important. But perhaps setting specific time aside to minister specifically to the children could be added.

How incredible to hear that the powerful Benny Hinn is now holding services specifically for youth and speaking into the lives of our young people. Glory to God! He's hearing from the Spirit! Another well-known minister, Luis Pulau, has been doing the same in recent years. I know of other ministers perhaps lesser known, such as Bob Jones, who will go into a church for a couple of days, and specifically request one service with the children. They are setting a tremendous example, which needs to be followed by hundreds more.

Keep in mind, we're looking for answers as to why there is such disinterest in God and spiritual things in kids born and raised in the Church, and why we are losing them by the droves. We must redefine children's ministry for the 21st century and all our traditions, habits, and mindsets have to be laid out on the table and discussed as potential areas for change.

"Tricked" into Children's Ministry

The call of God is an interesting thing. I know what it is like to feel the incredible pull in my spirit to serve Him. There were many years when to my leaders there seemed to be no indication that I was ministry material as far as being fivefold was concerned. Yet I remember thinking repeatedly in those days, "Brother Kenneth Hagin himself cannot possibly feel any more called to the ministry than I do." It was in me, even if it wasn't evident to others. But the thought that I was called to children didn't enter my mind for many years. The truth was, I jokingly tell people God "tricked me" to get me into working with kids.

When Jesus said, "The fields are white unto harvest and the laborers are few," (John 4:35) never was it more truly spoken of than over ministry to children.

I got involved in children's ministry purely because no one else would do it. I simply saw the need. I became righteously indignant that not even the pastor seemed to care about children's ministry in our church because we went for two years without any. (By the way, that was a erroneous perception on my part.) So with a bit of an attitude I took on the task. Therein, I collided with my destiny.

Bill Wilson, the incredible children's minister who serves twenty thousand children every week in the ghettos of New York City, says the same thing. He never felt God call him to children's ministry specifically. He simply saw the need and stepped up to the challenge. Some readers may recognize the names of other well-known children's ministers such as Willie George, John Tasch, Jim Wideman, and others. Their stories are similar. It was never a remote consideration for them to work with kids. But through various circumstances, they found themselves ministering to children, and realized that was where their true calling was.

Are You Sure You're in the Right Place in Ministry?

I can't help but wonder how many fivefold ministers have taken pastorates or are traveling ministers in whatever capacity, and somehow they missed their true calling to work with kids. Why do I say this? Because of the six and half billion people on the face of the earth, one third of them are under the age of nineteen. I really find it hard to believe with all those kids out there that God has not called more of His people to serve in children's ministry. When Jesus said, **"The fields are white unto harvest and the laborers are few,"** (John 4:35) never was it more truly spoken of than over ministry to children.

It's a fascinating thing to talk to Christians and hear them lament, "I just don't know where I fit in the body of Christ. I just wish I knew what my calling was!" We quickly tell them, "Well, we're in need of children's ministers!" They quickly retreat saying, "Sorry! I'm not called to children's ministry!" Isn't it funny? They don't know what they are called to, but they sure know what they're not called to!

The point is I believe with all my heart there are fivefold ministers "out there" who belong in children's ministry that for one reason or the other have yet to discover their true call. Let this be a challenge to seek the face of God on this issue, Fellow Minister. (Is your heart pounding a little faster right now? Sit up and take notice! We need you!)

Missionaries and church planters, reconsider what you're doing and where you're putting your effort! Open your eyes and see the obvious— everywhere you go overseas you're tripping over kids. This represents a gigantic need in the body of Christ!

Are Children's Pastors Fivefold?

The head pastor of a church one time told me matter-of-factly that children's ministers were not fivefold ministry gifts because they weren't listed in Ephesians 4:11. Somewhat stunned by his thinking, I immediately asked him why he would let anyone minister to his children on a regular basis if he did not believe they were fivefold. Yet I would guess this is common thinking among leaders. I would venture to say it never occurs to the typical head pastor in the process of hiring to try to determine whether his children's ministers are authentic fivefolders or not. In fact, I don't know of very many, if any, head pastors or church elders that even consider this as criteria at all in hiring children's pastors. We tend to look for clowns, puppeteers, good entertainers, or great administrators who like kids. Do we ever investigate whether or not our children's pastors are legitimate fivefold ministry gifts? Does it matter?

Yes, it's important that head pastors and more experienced, well-known ministers reach out to today's children. But it's equally important that the people we hire and place directly over these kids walk in some type of fivefold ministry for the very same reasons we've already named. There's been a trend over the last couple decades to hire "Christian Education Directors" who basically oversee the educational programs for all ages in local congregations. But, in all due respects, children need their own pastor if they are going to be truly "pastored" as well as equipped for the ministry according to Ephesians. It is just as important for this person to be a bonified fivefold minister as it is for the head pastor.

In Conclusion

The truth is, for many legitimate reasons, a significant number of our children's ministries are run by volunteers within the congregations who are not technically five-folders. The question we need to ask ourselves is, is it even possible for these precious laborers to equip children in the sense that we're talking about if they are not naturally gifted by the Spirit of God to do so? And is it important?

The last thing we would ever want to do is make the thousands of hard-working, caring, committed children's workers feel like they are unqualified or unable to impact our children as workers in our local churches because they aren't fivefold ministers. Nothing could be further from the truth! **We are all called to make disciples, not just fivefolders, and it would be unfair for Jesus to require us to do something that was impossible for us to do!** To say one cannot have a positive, even powerful, influence on the lives of children if they are not in this category would be to negate the fruit of every teacher who has turned the lives of hundreds of students around because of their influence.

The answer is a resounding "Yes!" They can wonderfully equip children as long as they have the training and support of their pastors to encourage and stand along side of them. All we are saying in this chapter is that there is a special importance fivefold ministers have in all of our lives, including the children. As head pastors and other ministers begin taking a more specific interest in their children's ministries, begin speaking into the lives of the children in the congregations, and recognize their own importance as the spiritual fathers of the house, this will take us to another level in redefining children's ministry in the 21st century!

Taking Action

1. If you are the head pastor of your church, how do you feel about the idea of becoming personally involved in ministering to your kids?

_____

_____

_____

2. If you are already involved, describe what you feel has been the impact on the children of your church.

_____

_____

_____

3. What are some ways you feel you could encourage the other leaders of your church to become involved in mentoring children?

_____

_____

_____

Most church going parents are neither
spiritually mature nor spiritually inclined and
therefore they do not have a sense of
urgency or necessity about raising their kids
to be spiritual champions.

The Role of Parents in Discipling Children

Changing Our Perspective

The whole issue of parents becoming spiritual trainers and disciplers of their own children is absolutely huge, and to a very large degree the universal Church is doing very little to intentionally equip them in this regard. In many cases, it's not even on the Church's radar screen. I personally have to admit my entire perspective in this book has been from that of the present day church culture where somehow over the years we've evolved into believing this was the job of the local church.

Separating kids into their own classes has generally become standard procedure so the parents and other adults (including pastors) can "get something out of the adult services" without distraction. If we're honest, we have to say this has often been more the issue than concern for the spiritual development and welfare of the children. In fact, I remember being told by my leaders it was not an option to cancel children's services because of a few parents who wouldn't bother coming to church due to the hassle of struggling with their own children in the adult service, even for special meetings. Thankfully, however, we are beginning to see more and more parents who are wanting to reverse this trend and play more of a role in their children's spiritual lives.

The Biblical Formula

Though I am still an advocate of children being ministered to on their level at least some of the time for a number of reasons, if we are truly going to truly redefine children's ministry in the 21st century, we can not ignore the critical role parents must play as the primary disciplers of their own children.

No doubt a big majority of children's ministers would agree they can easily recognize the difference between the spiritual maturity and development of children who are raised in families who are working with them in the home and those who are not. This is not an accident. It's actually the biblical formula. On the one hand we have almost worn out scriptures like **"train up a child in the way he should go,"** (Proverbs 22:6). Yet on the other hand we have lost sight that this implies the role parents, not churches, are to play in their child's spiritual upbringing.

The whole issue of parents becoming spiritual trainers and disciplers of their own children is absolutely huge, and to a very large degree the universal Church is doing very little to intentionally equip them in this regard.

There's a lot of talk in some Christian circles about going back to the way "they did things in the Bible days." While some of those ways may not be practical in our western culture, the issue of how children were trained and mentored by Jewish parents deserves some serious attention. Almost everything children learned was taught to them by their parents in the home, even the family trade. When it came to the nation of Israel holding corporate prayer and fasting sessions, the Scriptures say they took their children with them to participate.

"But even now," declares the LORD, "return to me with all your heart— with fasting, crying, and mourning." Tear your hearts, not your clothes. Return to the LORD your God…Schedule a time to fast. Call for an assembly. Gather the people. Prepare them for a holy meeting. Assemble the leaders. Gather the children, even the nursing infants." (Joel 2:12-16 GWT)

The book of Deuteronomy is liberally sprinkled with references to telling parents how to raise their children as worshipers of God. On the other hand there are no instructions about dropping the children off at church once a week to get their spiritual education. Rather the scripture is entirely full of instructions for parents to take on this responsibility themselves on a daily basis in the home. But herein lies the challenge.

Today's Parents Feel Inadequate

When the average Christian parent feels inadequate and ill equipped to disciple their children in spiritual issues, the best they know to do is take them to a church with a good children's program.[2] In fact, it's interesting to note that finding a good children's ministry is very near the top of list in why families choose a church to attend regularly. I've wondered how they determine what a good program is when all they know to do for their children is what was modeled before them, which may or may not be much.

The point is, they want their children involved in a good children's ministry, whatever that is in their minds. George Barna makes an interesting observation and a very strong statement when he writes, "Most church going parents are neither spiritually mature nor spiritually inclined and therefore they do not have a sense of urgency or necessity about raising their kids to be spiritual champions. Most parents believe that enabling their children to attend church on a regular basis and to feel generally positive about their religious experience is as high as they can set the bar. Anything achieved beyond that level is seen as a bonus."[3]

This leaves a heavy, and unnatural, responsibility on our shoulders as children's ministers, because we are then the ones who must decide what it will take to make children into spiritual champions. Though we all know of parents who are very engaged in their children's spiritual lives, it's also possible, in other cases, we might be the only ones who are passionate about how far our kids go in spiritual things. Hopefully this book has been a help to you in clarifying what direction to take in raising spiritually mature kids. However, it doesn't mean the parents of our children will have the same aspirations and values. Many times, they don't even know what standards they are supposed to have. This leaves us as church leaders in the awkward position of needing to help guide the parents.

The last thing we want is an arrogant attitude that we know what's better for other people's children than they do. This is not the point of what we're doing here. This is a situation where some parents are expressing a feeling of inadequacy in this arena, so we are trying to help them. This may not be the way God originally planned it, but it seems to be the situation we are faced with. Our role technically should be that of supporting and reinforcing what the parents are trying to accomplish with their children at home. But it seems our roles have been somewhat reversed as it relates to spiritual issues.

According to Barna, "Parents across the nation admit one of the greatest benefits they receive from attending church is having their community of faith assume responsibility for the spiritual development of their children. Knowing that there are trained professionals and other willing individuals who will provide spiritual guidance to their children is a source of security and comfort for most churchgoing adults."[4] The message to children's ministers here is parents really do want our help. We need to do everything we can to guide them into what they can do to take the spiritual leadership and responsibility in the lives of their children.

> "Their virtual abandonment of spiritual leadership for their children is evident in how infrequently they engage in faith-oriented activities with their young ones."[5]

Abandoning Spiritual Leadership

Barna continues writing, "Our national surveys have shown that while more than four out of five parents (85%) believe they have the primary responsibility for the moral and spiritual development of their children, more than two-thirds of them abdicate that responsibility to their church. Their virtual abandonment of spiritual leadership for their children is evident in how infrequently they engage in faith-oriented activities with their young ones. For instance, we discovered that in a typical week, less than one out of every ten parents who regularly attend church with their kids read the Bible together, pray together other than at meal times, or participate in an act of service as a family unit. Even fewer— less than one out of every twenty—have any type of worship experience together, other than while they are at church, during a typical month."[5]

This is really an eye opener and may explain a lot to us about some of the challenges we've faced with trying to create a spiritual hunger in the children of our ministries. Very few people, adult or child, can go with nearly zero interaction with the Lord during the week, then walk into church Sunday morning ready to jump into deep worship and desire for the Word. We all must nurture our relationships with the Lord regularly to keep us in a state of hunger and wanting more of Him.

It's unclear from Barna's statement whether or not these are parents who have their own strong devotional life apart from their children. You may be surprised, however, to hear your head pastor say he faces the same challenge in trying to encourage the adults of their church to spend time with the Lord themselves during the week. If that is the case, we have a double battle: 1) get the parents motivated to seek God for themselves through prayer, worship, and Bible study in their homes, then 2) getting them motivated to do the same thing with their children.

Family Ideas for Spiritual Activities

Encouraging parents and children to share their devotional lives together will greatly enable them to enhance their spiritual influence on their children. With this in mind, you may want to think of ways to share this with your parents, giving them ideas of what they can do together as a family. There are actually a number of books that have been written on this very subject, in case your parents don't know where or how to begin. We list some of them in the "Notes" section at the end of the book.

Praying and spending time reading the Word together (which may be reading Bible story books or children's devotional books depending on the age of the child) are just the more obvious ways parents and children can interact together. But in other homes, children may resent the "sit still" time. In those cases you will want to find other creative ideas and exciting ways to do related types of things. This is where the books we mentioned would be very helpful. But I can tell you from personal experience, children who have parents who are working with them in some way spiritually in the home are more open to the things of God in my services than those who don't. It makes sense. Whatever parents place a priority on, the children will have more of a tendency to value as well.

> Ideally, the goal of seeing children become spiritual champions will become the parents' vision and they will begin to get an idea of what kind of spiritual standards they should have for their boys and girls.

Share Your Vision With the Parents

The job of how to begin bringing our parents into their rightful place as spiritual leaders in the home will be challenging and a long term goal. It actually needs to be part of the vision of the whole church, and not just the children's ministry department! As you become secure and convinced about the direction you want it to go spiritually with your kids, it would be very helpful if you let the parents know what your priorities and vision are. This will hopefully help them get a picture of what it is they should desire for their children spiritually, especially if there is a way to encourage parents to reinforce what you're doing at home.

In very practical ways, you might do this in the form of a brochure handed out or mailed to each family. You may choose to do a monthly or quarterly newsletter for parents and grandparents. Or you may choose to have a meeting, perhaps a meal together with the parents, in which you can share your heart in how you would like to see their children develop, casting vision for what their children's spiritual potential really is. You may even ask your pastor if you might address the congregation two or three times a year for ten minutes to share your vision for the children of your church. Ultimately as you make progress in the training of your kids, you may even ask the pastor for opportunities for them to minister to the congregation in some way. Seeing is believing and understanding!

The point is in some way the parents need to be informed of what it is you hope to accomplish with their children, especially as you begin this new adventure of equipping children for the work of the ministry. Ideally, the goal of seeing children become spiritual champions will become their vision and they will begin to get a picture of what kind of spiritual standards they should have for their boys and girls. It may even cause them to hunger for more of God in their own lives.

Experiment With New Ideas

Helping parents begin to take ownership of their children's spiritual training is something most of us in church leadership are still experimenting with. Recently in a local children's ministry I lead during the week, we worked hard encouraging parents and grandparents to attend the meetings along with their children, making them intergenerational services. Though the content is still geared for the children, I am actively looking for ways for the parents and children can interact with each other rather than just sitting and listening to me talk.

For instance, one week our lesson was on praise. We asked everyone to gather into family groups. (We made sure all children had a group to go to if there parents were not there.) We asked the parents to look up various Psalms with their children, together finding as many things as possible which we should praise God for. In another service I asked for the parents to cluster with their children and share their testimonies of how they became Christians. Most children have never heard thes stories before, and it is as important for them to know this about their parents as it is to know about their secular family history.

In many of my meetings we all come together to the front to pray. In some cases it is for world missions, or sometimes for specific people we know. We encourage everyone to contribute a prayer, a word of knowledge, a mini-vision they may have gotten during prayer, and so on. These are often our most powerful services—all generations working together to stand in the gap for others. The purpose is to hopefully open the parents thinking to various ways they can to be personally involved in their children's spiritual lives and get families used to doing spiritual things together.

> We ultimately want the parents to gain the urgency and necessity about raising their kids as spiritual champions that many of them feel they are now missing.

In Conclusion

In the process of redefining children's ministry in the 21st century, there must be a fresh partnership between parents and the church. A friend of mine who leads a children's prayer team told me, "My most spiritual intercessors are the ones whose parents are involved in their spiritual training at home." We need to remember the importance of training and equipping parents to continue at home what we have tried to do in our services with their kids. We must somehow give them the tools, confidence, and understanding to continue the spiritual process in the daily lives of their children. We can begin by helping make parents aware of the spiritual potential of their children. As we children's ministers and leaders begin to view kids as significant spiritual beings, we can then show parents how they can help teach their children to walk in the supernatural as well at home, school, and play. This is going to require a new approach to how we conduct children's ministry, but in doing so we will continue to redefine children's ministry in the 21st century.

Taking Action

1. *What do you think the level of awareness is of the parents in your church of their role in the spiritual discipling of their own children?*

_____

_____

_____

2. *What are some ways you can begin helping parents realize they need to set spiritual goals for their children?*

_____

_____

_____

3. *What are some things you can do in your ministry to involve the parents in the spiritual lives of their children?*

_____

_____

_____

Musicians need to consider the possibility that they might be called to children's ministry. With the billions of kids in the world, surely some of the kazillion musicians in the Church are called to the children.

Musicians & Children's Ministry

Musical Woes

Music, that is, praise and worship continues to be a conundrum in children's ministry. The quality of the music in churches in adult services is one of the most important issues as people "shop" for churches and choose church homes. We've been made aware of and quickly spoiled by incredibly powerful praise and worship available by either radio, TV, CDs, concerts, or tapes available in Christian bookstores or on the Internet. To say the least, Christians like their praise and worship. You can almost endure a poor sermon in a service if the music is good enough!

But finding good Christian music for children is a challenge. Finding good praise and worship in a children's service is an even greater challenge. Until recently, the only kind of really good music you could find was suitable only for kids ages eight and under. In that category, it seems awesome music abounds. But for the older kids—the "tweeners"—frankly, there's not a lot out there. There have been a few companies that have risen to the challenge and produced some really good products, but more needs to be made. Anyone who is even remotely in touch with this present generation knows how vitally important music is to them in the secular arena. It just stands to reason it would also be this way in the Christian world. The music we sing as children will be the music we sing in our old age. It's vital now and for the future to have good, Christ-honoring music for our children.

Those of us in children's ministry realize good quality music in a children's service is just as important as it is for an adult service. In most cases, we've had to become masters at producing anointed, flowing, quality praise and worship for our services from CDs and DVDs because of the scarcity of live musicians available to us. It can be done to a point, but it definitely has its challenges.

But in redefining children's ministry in the 21st century, we really need to make an appeal to the hundreds of thousands of Christian musicians who feel called to do praise and worship. Musicians need to consider the possibility that they might be called to children's ministry. In an earlier chapter I said I find it difficult to believe not more fivefold ministers have been called to children's ministry because of the billions of kids on the face of the earth. My point was that with such a huge number of kids, it was hard to believe God wasn't drawing more people in to minister to them. In the same way, and for the same reasons, I also have a hard time

Kids are just as capable of going into the throne room of God in worship as adults are, and even hunger to do so.

believing that with the kazillions of musicians in our ranks that more of them aren't called to praise and worship for children.

There's a desperate need for this in the body of Christ, whether it is producing good tapes and CDs, or helping as live musicians in children's services. There are very few children's ministries I know of who have the luxury of live musicians committed to doing the kids' music on a regular basis. Larger churches seem to have an advantage in this bcause of sheer numbers, but not in the average children's ministry in the average church. Likewise, I only know of a handful of traveling musicians who are committed to children's ministry and serious praise and worship for kids.

Kids Love Deep Worship

Some of the reasons there are not more live musicians in churches are very practical. Some churches choose to keep their children in the main sanctuary for the adult praise and worship. In some cases, the facilities are not conducive to live music with all of the space needed for instruments, etc. Many children's ministries cannot afford adequate sound systems a live band requires, much less having people who know how to run the equipment. But we need to understand that for whatever reason, children seldom reach their full potential in praise and worship if the only thing they are ever exposed to is an adult praise and worship service or CDs.

In one of the churches I pastored, we kept our kids in the adult worship for years. But once we began having our own praise and worship strictly among ourselves, our kids took off spiritually to a much greater degree, in spite of being handicapped musically for lack of live musicians.

Still another practical problem is that churches may be limited in the number of quality musicians they have available even for the adult services. This is especially true in smaller churches. But I was a part of a larger congregation where musicians were almost a dime a dozen, and even then there was no one who was willing to commit to the children's services more than once a month. They didn't want to miss the chance to play in the adult band. I was thankful to have them when I could, but it was very difficult to build a consistent flow in praise and worship with a different set of musicians every week with diverse styles of music.

How Kids' Worship is Perceived

It is possible that one reason there are not more live musicians committed to children is because of the way it is perceived—as having no spiritual depth. Musicians understandably want to go into the deep praises of God and stay there as long as possible. There's something about being able to usher in the overwhelming presence of God into a building full of people, and it's seldom the image we have when thinking about children's services. But let it be known, kids are just as capable of going into the throne room of God in worship as adults are and hunger to do so.

In fact, there have been times I have felt the presence of God stronger in children's meetings than in many average Sunday morning church services. When they're trained, kids can get very lost in worship. I remember one Sunday morning as a children's pastor where we hit such a pocket of worship we absolutely could not pull the kids out of it. They refused to quit and go into the next portion of the service. We captured it on video tape, and every now and then I go back and watch it. I'm just as amazed each time I view it at how those kids just did not want to leave the presence of God. There were other times on a Sunday morning service where the kids were the last ones to leave the church, and parents literally had to come and drag their kids away from His presence as we worshiped. I might add, in every one of those occasions we just happened to have the privilege of live musicians. I often wondered where we could have taken the kids spiritually if we could have had consistent powerful music each week.

> Children do not necessarily gravitate to worship automatically just because of what they've observed in adult worship. They are wired differently.

I Will Become More Undignified Than This

One of the things children's ministry is known for is action choruses. Kids absolutely love it, and they need it. When done right, it can be just as anointed as conventional praise and worship. Taking the contemporary songs and putting actions and dance steps to them can be powerful! The presence of God can fill the room with absolute joy in this form of praise! It can also usher in a wave of prophetic intercession, even spiritual warfare! Perhaps we all need to be challenged by the song that says, "I will become even more undignified than this!" especially if it will take the children higher in the spirit. It can feel very undignified at times to be waving your arms wildly, bending high and low, and Lord only knows what other actions that come with it. But something happens to the atmosphere when we step into this form of worship and the songs have powerful Christ glorifying lyrics. God shows up in a unique way.

An Acquired Taste

Children do not necessarily gravitate to worship automatically. In some ways it's an "acquired taste" for them. But it usually has to do with what they've observed in the adult worship services. They are wired differently than adults, and just like in their sermons, they have different needs and tastes.

For instance, the typical adult songs have far too many lyrics for them. You need to select songs that are "kid friendly." For a song to be singable and enjoyable to a child, they need to have few words, and need to be repetitious. When the song is simple, they can then begin to sing along, and it becomes enjoyable. Quite often the chorus of a popular song is easy for them, but the verses overwhelm them because they are so full of words.

So at the very most, it's best to sing only one verse, and do it over and over again along with the chorus, rather than all of the verses of the song. Then kids can learn it. When a song is easy to sing and becomes familiar, it's then they can be taken into the presence of God more easily and with less resistance. This again is something that is much easier to do with live musicians as opposed to CDs because they have the option of changing things to make the songs simpler.

An additional important issue to remember is to not use "childish" or "babyish" songs especially where older kids are present. This is very demeaning to them. I'm sorry, but *Father Abraham*, while being fun and cute does not usher in the presence of God! Stick with mature music that even adults would enjoy.

Mentor, Train, Equip

As in any other area, children have to be mentored and guided as to what to do in worship. Just because they've seen the adults raise their hands and close their eyes a thousand times in the adult service, doesn't mean they will necessarily copy them without encouragement. Even then, they need to be given reasons why they should raise their hands, or close their eyes. What's the point? Never hound or force children to do these things. Simply give them good practical reasons why they are helpful, and how they contribute to your goals of getting into the presence of God.

Set a good example for them. Teach a little bit on worship each week. Give them new things to think about and do in each service so it doesn't become predictable and boring. For instance, one week emphasize bowing and kneeling before the throne. The next, wave flags and banners worshipfully in honor of the King. Another week dance with arms upraised and eyes looking to the sky. Ask the Lord to help you be creative in this portion of your service so it becomes a time to look forward to. Finally, don't worry about repeating the same songs week after week. The more familiar the children are with the songs, the more they can freely enter in. This doesn't mean you should never introduce new songs. But you shouldn't try to sing new songs every week.

> Our desire for our children should be to give them every conceivable advantage to go as far in the Spirit as it is possible to go. This will have to include music.

In Conclusion

If we're going to complete the full spectrum of redefining children's ministry in the 21st century, we're going to have to address the issue of music. Kids need to learn how to worship the living God, and they can do it if someone takes the time to teach them. They need to know what to do and why they are doing what they do. They won't automatically fall into it. It doesn't necessarily come naturally for them. But they can learn.

I'm just radical enough to believe we need to give our kids the best—the best preachers, the best teachers, the best prophets, the best evangelists, the best apostles, and, yes, even the best musicians. We have to stop giving our kids the "second string" in every area. If this is truly the generation all the prophets are declaring will usher in the Second Coming of Jesus, we've got to become fanatically obsessed with equipping them with the best of everything.

Our desire for our children should be to give them every conceivable advantage to go as far in the Spirit as it is possible to go. This will have to include music—live praise and worship. It's going to have to involve a fresh wave of singers, song writers, and musicians willing to spend themselves on wiggly, freckle-faced children. We must lean fully on the Holy

Spirit to take us into the Holy of Holies, and with the help of skilled musicians we will be able to catapult them where we need to go with this generation in billows of praise and worship. Please, musicians, will you help us redefine children's ministry in the 21st century?

Taking Action

1. *As a children's minister, how important do you feel praise and worship has been in your services?*

_____

_____

_____

2. *How do your children feel about praise and worship? What can you do to improve their attitude if needed?*

_____

_____

_____

3. *If live musicians are not an option for you, what's the next best thing you can do to improve worship in your services right now?*

_____

_____

_____

Part Two:
The Process

Every command Moses had ever given was
read to the entire assembly, including the
women and CHILDREN*...
Joshua 8:35 (NLT)

(*Emphasis is mine)

It's Time to Begin

Ready! Set! Go!

We've spent a great deal of time outlining the reasons behind the need of redefining children's ministry in the 21st century in the first half of this book. But it may have seemed like a lot of "theory" to you at this point. You may still be wondering what does a children's ministry that encompasses all these areas really look like? If you've never seen children prophesying, or laying hands on the sick, etc. you may be full of questions.

Everybody's ministry will look differently based on areas of strength, interest, anointing, and the people you have available to help you in your church. But in the following chapters, we outline various ideas that I have personally used in my own ministries, and those I have observed from other children's ministers who have been actively equipping children in their own spheres of influence. These should help you be able to visualize how to set your goals, and even give you some very practical methods to do similar things in your own church.

After teaching these principles in one church, parents and children's workers alike kept telling me, "I just didn't know it was that easy!" And it really is easy to activate children in the works of Jesus. I truly hope by reading these next chapters that it will take all of the mystery out of this concept for you. I pray you will be able to grab hold of the vision of raising up a generation of evangelists, prophets, apostles, and radical, on fire worshipers who will not be afraid of spreading the gospel to the ends of the earth! As you begin stepping out, you will be joining the ranks of many thousands who are helping to redefine children's ministry in the 21st century! Ready! Set! Go!

Next to their salvation, there is not another subject more important for them to be taught than the subject of the baptism in the Holy Spirit.

Children & the Holy Spirit

Beginning at the Beginning

I am continually dumbfounded as I travel around the USA and the world at how few of the children being raised in charismatic and Pentecostal churches are filled with the Holy Spirit. If they don't get it in our churches, and the parents feel ill-equipped to lead them in it, where are they going to get it? And if not in childhood, then when? As I will detail later in this chapter, the longer we wait to lead a child into this experience, the less chance there is they will ever receive this precious gift.

Next to their salvation, there is not another subject more important for them to be taught than the subject in the baptism in the Holy Spirit. Jesus said we needed this experience and made a big point about instructing the disciples to go to Jerusalem and wait for the promise of the Father. He did not say, "Everyone over twenty-one needs this experience," or "All moms and dads should have it." He said every believer needs to be filled with the Holy Spirit.

If adults need it, then so do kids. In fact, He specifically said in Acts 2:39, **"For the promise is unto you, *and to your children*,** [emphasis mine] **and to all that are afar off, even as many as the Lord our God shall call."** Just before He ascended into heaven, He told his disciples, **"These signs shall follow *them that believe*** [emphasis mine]**…they will speak with new tongues."** If children are believers, this is one sign that should be following them. According to scripture, if a child can be saved, then he/she can be filled with the Holy Spirit.

I am really not sure why this subject is so down played or avoided in so many charismatic churches in America these days. But it needs to be revived and brought to the forefront once again, because therein lies the power for life and miracles.

As a child and young adult I belonged to what is now the largest Pentecostal denomination in the world. Just a few years ago their leader publicly shared that only 25% of their members were filled with the Holy Spirit with the accompanying ability to speak in tongues. I was stunned. As I child, it was this very subject that got us the "left foot of fellowship" with all the other denominations in town. It was our identifying mark. It was what uniquely set us apart in the body of Christ. To hear it is becoming all but extinct in this circle was really quite a crushing blow to me. (By

> If they don't get it in our churches, and the parents feel ill-equipped to lead them in it, where are they going to get it? And if not in childhood, then when?

the way, this is totally the opposite of what is happening in other nations around the world. In fact, even among mainline denominations, a significant number of their adherents speak in tongues. There are almost as many Charismatics in other nations as there are mainline Christians, although unfortunately the issues seem to be the same in regards to bringing children into this experience.)

As we continue redefining children's ministry in the 21st century and beyond, it is imperative this topic be at the very top of the list of things needing to be changed in the way we currently minister to children.

Reasons Children Should be Filled with the Spirit

Because of the lack of attention this typically receives in many of our children's ministries, we need to rehearse the biblical purposes of the importance of being filled discussing specifically one of the accompanying signs, that of speaking in tongues. Allowing for differences of beliefs among charismatics and Pentecostals, we are taking the approach here that tongues is a significant part of the experience, believing there are also other signs of the infilling. But it appears from the following scriptures speaking in tongues is a supernatural experience that comes with some very specific benefits, which is what we want to address.

There are two sides to the issue of speaking in tongues as a part of the experience of being filled—a personal side, and a public side. We're dealing here with the personal benefits for the individual believer, although children can be used in a public setting as well. Let's see if any of the following areas would be valuable for children. For a more complete study on this subject, I recommend reading *Ten Reasons Why Every Believer Should Speak in Tongues* by Kenneth E. Hagin.[1]

1. *"You shall receive power when the Holy Spirit has come upon you, and you shall be witnesses to me..."* (Acts 1:8). Do children need power in their lives? The power is for many reasons. It's as much to overcome temptation and sin as it is to boldly and unashamedly spread the good news of Jesus Christ. Do children need to overcome sin and temptation? This is certainly a 'yes.' Are they responsible to tell others about Jesus? If they are truly followers of Jesus, they are according to Jesus. It's part of being one of His disciples.

2. *"He who speaks in tongues edifies himself..."* (1 Cor. 14:4) and *"building yourself up on your most holy faith, praying in the Holy Spirit..."* (Jude 20). "Building yourself up" basically means to edify yourself. Edify means to morally or spiritually uplift. Do children ever become depressed or discouraged? Would there ever be a reason a child would need to be edified, uplifted, or strengthened in his inner man? If so, then he should be encouraged to pray in tongues.

3. *"For with stammering lips and another tongue He will speak to this people, To whom He said, "This is the rest with which You may cause the weary to rest," And, "This is the refreshing"* (Isa. 28:11-12). Do children ever become weary with life and circumstances? Is there ever a time when they could benefit from resting in the Lord and being refreshed in His presence? If so, they would benefit from praying in tongues.

4. *"We hear them speaking in our own tongues the wonderful works of God."* (Acts 2:11, 1 Cor. 14:15-17) Praying in the spirit gives us an added edge in giving thanks and glorifying God. Should children give thanks and glorify God, and do they ever run out of words in their own language to do so like we do? If so, then they should know how to speak and worship in tongues.

5. *"Likewise the Spirit also helps in our weaknesses. For we do not know what we should pray for as we ought, but the Spirit Himself makes intercession for us with groanings which cannot be uttered,"* (Romans 8:26). Do children always know how to pray about things properly? Not even we adults know this. It's one of the important reasons we've been given tongues, so we know our prayers are lining up with the will of God in circumstances we don't understand in the natural. Then children, who have no tools yet to deal with the complicated world of adults, would benefit greatly by being able to be pure vessels whom the Holy Spirit can pray through.

Many children receive the Holy Spirit quietly and with little fanfare, yet it's a genuine experience. In other services, there is such an outpouring, the children weep and sob almost uncontrollably in the presence of God.

To Young to Understand

One of the most common criticisms I hear concerning children being filled with the Holy Spirit is that they are too young to understand what they're doing, or too young to understand what it's all about and therefore, they should not be filled. I love asking those same adults, "Are you telling me you actually understand this experience of speaking in tongues? Then please, explain it to me!" Nobody who's honest can say they can even remotely understand how you can speak a language fluently that you have never learned before, nor what is going on in the spirit realm while they're doing it.

Actually there are times I think the kids understand it better than we adults because they are not in the habit of letting their minds get in the way of what they are doing. Once they've been taught to flow with Him, they are very good at following His lead.

The first time I was confronted about this was from a parent who was almost irate that I would dare even bring up the subject to her nine-year-old son in our children's meetings. "He's too young!" she declared. After some discussion, and being assured from my pastor the church was in agreement with what I was doing, I basically told the mom if she didn't want her son to be filled with the Holy Spirit, she should not send him to our services. She backed down and said no more. The next few weeks when I preached on the subject and gave the children an opportunity to be filled, her son was one of the first ones to receive and speak in tongues.

It's Impossible to Make a Mistake!

It's important to remember how hungry children are for the supernatural, and this is one of the primary supernatural experiences they will ever have in their lifetimes. They move into these things so easily in most cases. Many children receive the Holy Spirit quietly with little fanfare, yet it's a genuine experience. In other services, there is such an outpouring the children weep and sob almost uncontrollably in the presence of God for as much as an hour or longer.

The first time this happened in one of my meetings, I was as shocked as anyone else at what transpired. About twenty-five kids, from preschoolers to teenagers, had come forward to say they wanted God to use them to do great things for Him. As they stood quietly at the altar, I was impressed to ask how many of them were filled with the Holy Spirit. Less than half raised their hands. So I immediately asked the others if they wanted to be filled, led them in a prayer, then said, "All right, begin speaking in tongues now."

As is fairly common, many of them stood there not knowing what to do next. I began laying hands on them one at a time, trying to take them further, when the Holy Spirit whispered to me, "Tell them it's impossible to make a mistake!" I began to shout this out repeatedly. Suddenly at the other end of the line there was a small rumble of voices, which exploded into shouting, hollering, weeping, and crying out. As I began walking up and down the line to see what had happened, the kids were totally lost in the presence of the Lord, completely oblivious that anyone else was in the room. With tears streaming down their faces, some on their knees, and others laid out on the floor, nearly all of them were speaking in tongues.

> I have found many times they are so hungry that it's not even necessary to lay hands on the kids individually. I just say "Now!" and the Spirit falls on them in an astounding fashion.

A Million Dollar Rain

I was so stunned at the display of emotion and the outburst they were making, I felt a little bit like Steve Irkle on the old TV sitcom *Family Matters* thinking, "Did I do that?" The Holy Spirit spoke to me the words, "This is a million dollar rain!" I knew from my upbringing in farm country exactly what He meant. It was much needed water on dry ground at just the right time to save the crop.

Later one of the mothers called me and talked about her small daughter who had been filled that night. The little girl told her mom, "Miss Becky told us it was impossible to make a mistake, so I decided to try, and it just happened!"

These days, though it never becomes common, it is a regular experience to see kids moved with tremendous emotion as they are baptized in the Spirit. Some children shake on the floor for hours under the power and demonstration of His presence. I have found many times they are so hungry that it's not even necessary to lay hands on the kids individually. We just take them into deep worship and presence of God, and I just say, "Now!" The Spirit falls on them in an astounding fashion. I never tire of seeing children completely wasted under the hand of God, melting in heaps of emotion on the floor in His presence when no human hand has touched them.

The Younger the Better

One of the interesting observations I've made over the years is the younger the child is, the easier it is for him to be filled with the Spirit. The older the child, the harder it is, even if they are being raised in Pentecostal or charismatic churches. Over and over again I've watched the preschooler be filled sooner than the twelve-year-old, and the newly converted child speak in tongues quicker than the child who's been raised in the church.

Several parents have told me their toddlers spoke in tongues before they spoke in English, their native language. Some friends of mine talked about one of their daughters riding in the booster chair in the back seat of their car at a time when she could only speak a few words of clear English. Both parents at the same time upon hearing their daughter chattering in unknown gibberish, looked at each other and asked, "Did you hear that?" They continued to listen, and it was clearly an unknown tongue and not just her typical childish chatter.

In my own personal experience having grown up in a Christian home, I can honestly say I have no idea when I was filled with the Holy Spirit. I do not remember any particular time or place when it happened for the first time, nor have my parents ever said they saw me go forward at any specific time to receive. I just know I grew up with the ability to pray in tongues. In fact, I went through a season as an older child where I really questioned if what I had was real because I had no specific experience to point to. I wasn't sure if I was making it all up or not. All I knew is that I could speak in tongues. I finally quit fighting it, and went on to enjoy it. I have met a number of other children who've had similar experiences.

It's important as adults that we do not carry any preconceived ideas about what a valid experience is for children. Do not expect them to have an "adult" experience like you did. If it happens fine, but don't box them in.

Preschool Is the Ideal Time

Preschoolers and the Holy Spirit is really a subject all its own. We don't have time to go into in a lot of detail about here. But after watching how completely open and sensitive these little ones are to the Lord, I've come to the conclusion the preschool ages and early grades are the ideal time to bring children into this experience. They are the least resistent because they have not yet entered the realm of trying to figure things out with their minds. They simply accept what you tell them.

We don't need to push them, nor try to force them to move on into this experience. We simply talk about it regularly as though it's a part of normal life, and make it available on an ongoing basis for "whosoever will" by our actions. You will be surprised how many of them will simple step over the line in their little preschool classes as Teacher begins to speak out in tongues during prayer and praise time. They may show no interest for weeks, then all of a sudden, you'll have a bunch of little guys and gals running around speaking in unknown languages while they're coloring their pictures.

> The preschool ages and early grades are the ideal time to bring children into this experience. They are the least resistent because they have not yet entered the realm of trying to figure things out with their minds.

The very first time I led a group of children into the baptism in the Holy Spirit, I didn't even know I was called into children's ministry. I was merely "taking my turn" in the children's department like all good adults did from time to time. But I had been priming the pump, and these kids were hungry for more of God. When I gave the call, about twenty boys and girls of all ages crowded around me. I led them in a prayer, and released them to begin speaking in tongues. This was the first time I noticed how difficult it was for the older kids who loved the Lord and had been raised in our church to step over the line and speak in tongues. However, most of them did eventually receive that morning. Buried in the middle of the crowd was a little blonde headed, blue-eyed boy named Kyle who was about four-years-old. When I looked at Kyle, his eyes were open, and he was chewing his gum and looking around at all the other kids. He wasn't making a disturbance or bothering anyone, so I left him alone, even though it didn't look like he was receiving anything.

At the end of the service, his mom came up to me and said, "Kyle tells me he got filled with the Holy Spirit today."

Confused I said, "No, he didn't. He just stood there popping his gum and looking at everyone else."

"Well," she smiled, "he says he can speak in tongues!"

I could hardly believe my ears, and went to hunt him down. When I found him I exclaimed, "Kyle! Your mom says you got filled with the Holy Spirit today. Is that true?"

"Uh huh," he nodded.

"Let me hear you speak in tongues!" I teased skeptically.

He immediately took off speaking fluently! It happened so fast, I didn't even have time to see it take place. I was amazed!

I highly recommend you educate your preschool teachers to talk about the Holy Spirit and demonstrate worshiping and singing in tongues regularly in their classes, without being pushy, and just see what happens. I believe you will be amazed at how easily they will be filled! Of course, we are assuming you're making ample opportunity for them to receive Jesus as Savior on a regular basis as well, which always comes first.

The Older, the More Challenging

The older child, on the other hand, is an entirely different matter. Those who have been raised around this experience have several different issues going on. First, they have watched this phenomenon for years in the adults and have never been able to figure out how everybody is doing it. If you ask them they will actually say, "I don't know how to do that." In other words, they are trying to figure it out with their intellect, and it can't be figured out. So they're stumped. No one has apparently ever taken the time to explain it to them. They have decided they can't do it.

Secondly, they see it as primarily an adult activity and have become used to the idea it's not for them, at least until they get older. They're not really sure what those grown-ups are doing or what excites them so much about this experience.

Thirdly, most of the time there's been no priority placed on it in their children's services, so there's been no need or hunger created for this experience. After all, they're saved, and doing fine without it, so why would they need it? No need. No hunger. Can't figure it out. It's primarily for these reasons, it seems, that the older the child who's been raised in the church, the harder it is for them to be filled with the Holy Spirit. If they once pass into their teen years without it, chances are slim they will receive somewhere down the line.

> In the same way we are to be salt in this world, causing people to become thirsty for Christ, children's appetites for the supernatural have to be stirred up, and, frankly, it seldom is in our children's ministries.

My Tanzanian friend Glorious Shoo, who has been a children's minister for years, was amazed the first time he came to this country and tried to lead a group of American children into the baptism. He said in his country, children receive immediately when he prays for them. But here, he was shocked at the lack of response of the church kids. After praying and pondering the situation for some time, he came to the conclusion there was little hunger for the experience, whereas in Africa, the children are desperate for God.

Newly Saved Kids Receive So Easily

This may seem like a contradiction to what I have been saying about how hungry children are for the supernatural. But keep in mind, in the same way we are to be salt in this world, causing people to become thirsty for Christ, children's appetites for the supernatural have to be stirred up. Frankly, this is seldom done in our children's ministries. It's not even an option that's been made available to them in many cases, so they don't know enough to be hungry for it. Their spirits need to be awakened to what's available to them and why. By contrast, when they watch a Harry Potter movie, or Saturday morning cartoons, they see the immediate benefits, or "the goods" of what the spirit world can do for them, and they seek after it. What are they ever shown in our churches? I would dare say, had Glorious gone into a group of heathen kids, and gotten them freshly born again, the response would have been completely different.

Hungry Native American Kids

This was made evident to me on the Ute Indian reservation during a week-long mission trip. I found out the third night out that it would be my job to do bus duty, going into the roughest community and riding with the kids by myself to the services. My first thought was what a challenge it had been the night before keeping crowd control with all the kids running in and out and I envisioned that those would be the kids who would end up on my bus. Not a pleasant thought!

But I found out when taking them home that night what softies they really were. It was a group of older kids about ten to twelve years old. The first night of our crusade most of them had the experience of being slain in the Spirit for the first time and kept saying they wanted to come back the next night and 'get knocked down' again. I decided to seize the moment and asked them if they had ever been filled with the Holy Spirit and spoken in tongues.

"You mean like those other kids did and like Pastor Fred does?" asked one little girl. (Pastor Fred, full blood Navajo, who pastors the only full gospel Indian church in the state of Utah, was our host pastor. These children had visited his church many times.) I told them yes, and they were hungry for everything God had for them. As I began to explain what it was, its purpose in our lives and how to receive, they crowded around my feet like a nest of baby birds with their mouths gaping open for heavenly food.

We laid our hands on their heads, led them in a prayer to receive, and five of the six instantly began speaking in their heavenly prayer languages. The rest of the half hour ride home all they wanted to do was speak in tongues or sing some of the songs they'd learned that night at the crusade.

A few years later in a tiny town in North Dakota, population 250, I had the unusual opportunity to minister the gospel for several weeks to the thirteen protestant elementary school kids, ages 8 to 12, with the blessing of the public school and their parents. All thirteen completely unchurched kids received Jesus the very first week I was with them, and were quick to tell me about the changes that had occurred in their lives as a

> He led them in a prayer, and the Holy Spirit poured out powerfully in the room. The children began to cry, weep, praying in tongues, and shouting so loudly it disturbed the whole school.

result. I had prayed in tongues over them a couple of times and explained what I was doing, but never felt led to teach on the subject. The last week I was there, I laid hands on each child and prayed over them before I left. Harlan, about ten years old, stood looking at me under his chocolate brown wavy hair, and captivating eyes. When I laid my hands on him, I had a knowing in my spirit he wanted to be able to speak in tongues too. I spoke to him, "Harlan, do you want to be filled with the Holy Spirit?"

He nodded yes, so excitedly, I began to explain a little more to him about it. I told him I was going to lead him in a prayer, and lay my hands on him, and….

While I was talking I looked at his lips which were moving rapidly, though he was making no sound. I stopped, smiled, and said, "You're already doing it, aren't you?" He just nodded and kept whispering in tongues. He was so open, I didn't even get a chance to pray for him. He simply received on his own!

Kids Receive in Public School

I received a fascinating report a couple of years ago from my friends in Tanzania regarding children being filled with the Holy Spirit in a public school in their city. Tanzania has a law on their books requiring all public schools to give one hour of religious instruction a week to all their students. It's a holdover from the days when Great Britain ruled their country. The government does not care what religion you teach, so Christians have an open door to preach the gospel. However, because of internal problems, such as no money to pay the teachers on occasion for a month or longer, teachers sometimes don't show up for classes.

Such was the case with this particular religion class. The students sat waiting patiently, but when no teacher arrived, an eleven-year-old boy proceeded to teach the other kids about the baptism in the Holy Spirit. At the end, he asked how many wanted to be filled, and all of them raised their hands. He led them in a prayer, and the Holy Spirit poured out powerfully in the room. The children began to cry, weep, and prayed in tongues, shouting so loudly it disturbed the whole school. (They don't have glass on their windows.) Teachers came running from everywhere to see what was the matter. One of the teachers who was a Roman Catholic nun decided the children were all demon possessed and was going to find a priest to cast the devils out.

But after about an hour, the children settled down. Finally they were able to tell the teachers what had actually happened. It was all because a young boy took the lead and followed his heart. The potential of children under the influence of the Holy Spirit is amazing.

In Conclusion

Being filled with the Holy Spirit with the accompanying ability to pray in tongues is fundamental to the supernatural life-style we want our children to step into. Before we could present chapters on prayer, healing the sick, or prophetic ministry, etc. this discussion was absolutely necessary. It should be such an automatic part of how we raise our children in the things of God that it should be as common place as offering salvation to them. But we hope this will forever change our attitudes toward bringing children into the infilling of the Holy Spirit and in doing so will fundamentally redefine children's ministry in the 21st century.

For he will be great in the sight of the Lord, and shall drink neither wine nor strong drink. He will also be filled with the Holy Spirit, even from his mother's womb.
Luke 1:15

Taking Action

1. Have you taught the children in your ministry on the baptism in the Holy Spirit within the last year? If not, why not?

_____

_____

_____

2. Would your children be able to tell you reasons why speaking in tongues is important? Would your adult helpers be able to?

_____

_____

_____

3. What are your personal concerns or the concerns of your parents or leadership about teaching children on this subject? What can you do to overcome these issues?

_____

_____

_____

It's very important to spend time building an expectation for the supernatural and creating a desire and hunger for this gift when there may have not been one up to this point.

Practical Guidelines in Leading Children into the Baptism

Facing Your Fears

M y greatest fear in leading children into the baptism in the Holy Spirit was, "What if I pray for them and nothing happens?" meaning, what if they don't speak in tongues? What will other people think? Isn't it interesting that we might be tempted to withhold this experience from them because of our own pride and what we might look like in front of other people? Then I was reassured by another children's minister with more experience than I how easily children received. I finally decided to try it. I decided to act more confident than I really was, and not let the children know I had any doubts about whether some would and others might not. I decided to boldly proclaim to them if they asked, God would be faithful to do it!

I also concluded, "We're down in the basement anyway. If I mess up and make a fool of myself, who's going to know it? Besides, kids don't know whether you're doing it right or wrong. So what have I got to lose? Let's try it!"

To my delight, I discovered what I really knew all along—it was not up to me anyway. God was either going to honor His Word, or it wasn't my problem. When I resigned myself to this, the pressure was off, and with each succeeding incident, I saw greater and greater results with the children. As long as I was confident, they were confident too. It's the same whether you're leading children or adults into the infilling of the Holy Spirit. I learned to always talk positive to the kids saying, "When you ask, you will receive!" We should never imply, "Some of you will get it, but maybe some of you won't." That's deadly to your desired outcome. They will believe what you say. You build expectation in them through your words.

Ask and Receive

There's really not a lot one needs to know about the actual process of leading someone into the baptism. The Bible pattern is fairly basic— you ask and you receive. What normally follows is speaking in tongues. The book of Acts does talk about the laying on of hands in the process, but it's not mandatory. Cornelius and his whole household began to speak in tongues while Peter was in the middle of his sermon. Obviously no one laid hands on them.

> If they don't have a solid understanding of why they should pray in this weird new way, they will not value the gift, and it will be lost to them either from misuse or no use.

What is extremely helpful with child or adult is some good teaching on the subject in advance. My least favorite time to bring children into the experience is "cold turkey" at the altar when I have not had a chance to preach or teach on the subject. So I rarely do that unless I really feel the leading of the Holy Spirit, as in the case with Harlan. Otherwise, it's very helpful to teach at least one sermon, if not more, on the subject so the children understand the real value of the experience, and what it is going to do in their lives.

Don't Be in a Hurry

We shouldn't be in a huge hurry to pray with them at the expense of laying a good solid foundation in our kids on this critical issue. It's very important to spend time building an expectation for the supernatural, and creating a desire and hunger for this gift when there may have not been one up to that point. I usually like to spend one whole session on who the Holy Spirit is, and the part He plays in our lives as Teacher, Guide, and Comforter. It's very valuable to spend one lesson on what Jesus had to say about it, and what happened at Pentecost.

I also find it very worthwhile to teach at least one whole class on speaking in tongues, if not more, because there is such misunderstanding about this gift. Children are very curious about it and have a zillion questions when it happens to them. Teaching on it in advance takes care of a lot of their questions up front. To me, it's almost unfair to expect them to speak in tongues when they know almost nothing about it or why it's important. If they don't have a solid understanding of why they should pray this weird new way, they will not value the gift, and it will be lost to them either from misuse or no use.

Keep Instructions Short and Sweet

When it comes time to actually leading them into the baptism, if you have done a good job of teaching, you need to keep your instructions at the altar short and simple. As with anything God has for us, there is no right or wrong way—no formula—of what to do. Most of the time I have the children respond to an altar call in the same way one would do for salvation. Then after the seekers have stepped to the front, I will call for other children who are already filled and can speak in tongues to circle around behind them for moral support.

I do this for a couple of reasons. One, I want the seekers to hear other children speaking in tongues rather than just adults so they will really know kids can do it, too. Second, I want to include the other children in the process so they will feel like God is using them, and so they will learn how to lead their friends into this experience down the road. We should never give our people the illusion that only the pastors, evangelists, or missionaries are qualified to do things like this. This is a part of the believer's ministry, and the earlier we train our kids to lead, the better off the whole body of Christ will be.

Remember—the job of leaders is to equip the saints to do the ministry! Our job as children's ministers is equipping the *little* saints!

Music Is a Powerful Helper

It's not absolutely necessary, but having good worship music playing really is helpful for setting a sweet atmosphere in the room. Since children's ministries seldom have the luxury of live bands, you will want to select a real powerful worship CD in advance, and just let it play in the background. It's really helpful if it's songs the children know and can sing along with to further usher in the presence of the Lord. It also helps to keep everybody focused. Yes, the Holy Spirit can move when it's silent, but when it's convenient, you should do everything you can to create an ambience where the presence of God can easily be felt. Also children are very shy when it comes to anyone hearing their voices in this initial stage. So having the music helps raise the noise level just enough that they don't feel so vulnerable in front of their friends.

> I personally do not equate the process of getting someone to make sounds in order to get them to speak out the same thing as "teaching" someone to speak in tongues.

Once everyone is in their places, ask the children to close their eyes for the purpose of being able to concentrate totally on the Lord and His goodness. Ask them to raise their hands in loving surrender to the Master, then lead them in a brief prayer asking God to fill them with His Spirit. I always like to lead them in a positive confession in the prayer saying something to the effect, "Thank you for the ability to speak in my new prayer language, and I believe I can do it now." This just helps build confidence and excitement for the supernatural.

Then I usually say something like, "On the count of three, we're all going to start praying in our prayer languages together. One, two, three, go!" I make sure everyone is praying nice and loud so the newcomers don't feel conspicuous. Normally, that's all it takes for most of the kids.

There will almost always be a few who are having a hard time stepping over the line, but you will soon notice those are kids who are really not even trying to speak in tongues. You'll notice no matter how often you tell them to open their mouths and say something, they will just stare at everyone else wide-eyed and mouths locked shut.

There's not a lot you can do about that until they are ready to step out. There will be others who are genuinely trying, but are still have a hard time breaking through. We try working with them, re-explaining things a few more times and just give them time.

Using Very Controversial Instructions

Every now and then, you will meet children who are genuinely hungry, and honestly trying to speak in tongues, but just don't seem to be able to break through. They are opening their mouths and trying to say something, but only their known language seems to still be coming out. My feelings on the issue are that most of them are still trying to figure it out with their heads, and it just isn't making any sense. They begin to get frustrated, feel stupid, and they begin to lose their confidence that anything is going to happen. As a last resort to get them started, I talk to them about how babies learn to talk. They just make sounds until one day the sounds take on a meaning, and they learn more and more sounds. None of the sounds make any sense, but it's talking to them until they learn what the sounds are connected to. I explain sometimes that's like speaking in tongues. We're making sounds that don't make sense, when suddenly those sounds just begin to flow out of our mouths without any effort. I encourage them to just begin making sounds and see what happens. Many times that's all it takes for the flow to begin.

However, if you do this, you need to know there are a lot of people who take great issue with it. The same mother who didn't want me teaching her nine-year-old son about the Holy Spirit, was also a little "testy" wanting to know if I was one of those people who "taught" kids how to speak in tongues. I've had numerous people ask me that same question since then. What they're trying to do is make sure the experience their child receives is genuinely supernatural and not humanly contrived.

But, of course, that's what we want too! What purpose would it serve for us to try to "manufacture" an experience like this for anyone? I personally do not equate the process of getting someone to make sounds in order to get them to speak out as the same thing as "teaching" someone to speak in tongues.

> When you send children, or anyone else, away from an altar who have not been successful in speaking in tongues, even if you really believe they didn't get filled, do them a favor and just don't say it to them.

It Backfired!

In one of my early experiences in this, I had a little boy about six years old who really loved the Lord, and truly desired to be filled with the Holy Spirit. But I had never met a child that young who simply was not able to speak in tongues. He really tried hard. In frustration, I told him to try to imitate some of the sounds he heard me or his parents making. But it backfired on me, and for the next fifteen minutes, all he would do was imitate my prayer language. He just never quite got it. I was at a loss as to what to do at that point, so we gave up for the night. I tried to assure him he had the ability and told his parents not to pressure him, but let it come naturally. Though a few years later he was finally able to speak in tongues, I have never asked anyone to repeat after me ever again.

To me, that would qualify more as trying to "teach" someone to speak in tongues, and it was not a good experience. I had used that technique on a couple of other people prior to this, and it worked just fine for them. They began speaking fluently in their own languages very quickly. But after that night with Shane, I just never tried it again. Instead, I began using the idea of making sounds similar to what a baby would make.

A Variety of Beliefs

It's not uncommon to have a child or two who just doesn't seem to be able to cross over into tongues. If you have a big group of children who've come forward to receive, you want to be careful not to drag the prayer time out too long because of one or two people. Unless there's an unusual move of the Spirit, I would try to keep the prayer time to about fifteen minutes unless they are all still very hooked up with what's happening. If you go too long, the other children get restless and inattentive, and the children having the trouble begin to feel awkward. You don't want to make a spectacle of them. Normally, I will encourage them and talk about some of the reasons people might have trouble speaking in tongues—none of which include God refusing to give it to them, *or that they did not get filled with the Holy Spirit.*

Here's where we get controversial again. There will be a wide variety of people with different beliefs reading this book. Some will even believe a person is not born again unless he speaks in tongues. The church I was raised in taught us that unless a person spoke in tongues, they were not filled with the Holy Spirit. I believed that way most of my life, but I don't personally accept this anymore. Please don't write me any letters to straighten out my doctrine. If you happen to be one who believes this, then let me just encourage you in something. When you send children, or anyone else, away from an altar who have not been successful in speaking in tongues, even if you really believe they didn't get filled, do them a favor and just don't say it to them. It serves no productive purpose, and actually discourages them making them feel either slighted by God or inadequate in some way, and they may not ever try again.

Get Alone With God

My encouragement is just send them home telling them, "When you get alone in bed, or in the bathtub, or in your playhouse in the backyard and it's just you and God, say, 'Now, Lord!' and see if you don't begin speaking in tongues." Some people just get very nervous and all tense in front of others. But when they get alone in a quiet place with the Lord, and the focus is off of them, they are able to relax and step right into the river. There have been many children who come back later to tell me when they got home they were able to then pray in tongues.

Jesus told us if we ask, we will receive. I believe if a person does not speak in tongues it's not God holding back the gift of the Holy Spirit. It's because there is something inside the person that is holding them back. It could be fear, insecurity, or feeling pressured. Some may have even been told in the past it's of the devil! I believe totally that when a person asks to be filled with the Holy Spirit, he instantly has the ability to speak in tongues, but that he is not always able to get it out. As soon as he can overcome his issues, tongues will be right there. In the same way our salvation is consummated when we confess to another human being that Jesus is our Lord, most people will never be completely satisfied with their experience of being filled until they're able to speak in tongues.

> Our children are in danger of never speaking in tongues after their first experience, if we don't lead and guide them otherwise.

Little Ears Are Listening

It's not unusual for some children's ministers to take kids who want to be filled into a side room and talk with them privately instead of in front of the whole group. Others will drop their voices in front of the responders and almost whisper so no one else can hear the instructions to them of what's going to happen next. I'm not sure why they do this, but I personally don't recommend either way. For one thing, it's important for all the children to be in on the process of seeing other children receive the Holy Spirit. It builds faith in them and an expectation for the miraculous. They need to become familiar and comfortable with it, and realize they need to be bold in their experience.

Once again, they need to see how it's done, so they can lead their friends into this experience. But even more than this, it's not at all unusual for kids sitting in the audience to hear the instructions you're giving to the kids up front and get filled sitting in their seats. They simply do what you've told the others to do and start speaking in tongues right where they are.

The first time this happened to me, once again a mother came to me after the service and said, "David told me he got filled with the Holy Spirit today." I thought for a moment, and said, "No, he didn't. He wasn't one of the kids who came forward for prayer."

"Well, I'm sure he said he can speak in tongues," she said creating a 'Déjà vu' moment for me. "I'll go ask him again."

When she returned, she told me David did indeed get filled, but that he simply didn't feel like going forward. He just followed my instructions while in his seat and received his prayer language. This has happened in my services several different times since then.

We Practiced Praying in Tongues

In my parents' generation, it was common to believe one could only speak in tongues when the Holy Spirit dropped on you with might and power. It usually involved goosebumps and electricity in the air and a very emotionally charged experience. Without these external feelings, they did not feel like they could speak in tongues. I knew a woman who had been filled and spoke in tongues when she was six years old. Hers was one of those outstanding experiences you never forget. But she never spoke in tongues again, because the same feeling never returned. She did not think she could or should.

Praise God, people don't believe this way today. However, our children are also in danger of never speaking in tongues after their first experience, if we don't lead and guide them otherwise. Many of the children in your ministry will go home to parents who are not filled with the Holy Spirit. They will never hear anyone in their home praying in tongues and therefore will seldom if ever be encouraged to do so there. Other children may have parents who are filled, but for whatever reason, they never pray in tongues in front of their children. If they have a private prayer time, they keep to themselves at that time, and the children once again never hear their parents praying in tongues, nor are encouraged to join in. Unless you as the children's pastor deliberately set aside time in each of your services to specifically pray in tongues, many of those kids will never do it again. That would be a shame.

On a regular basis, you need to rehearse with your children why tongues is valuable, and why they should make it a part of their lives. As often as possible, you should create times of worship when you say, "Okay, now we're going to worship the Lord in our prayer languages!" There should be other times when you pray for someone in your group, and the children should be encouraged to lay hands on them and pray for them in tongues as well as English.

Sometimes I simply made it a fun activity to make the point they were in control of this amazing gift and could speak in tongues any time they wanted to—playing with dolls, riding bikes, taking a bath, washing the dishes, or riding in a car. This was an attempt to make it a part of their daily life-style. At times, we would pray in one-minute intervals using our "playground voices" and the next minute using our "whisper voices." I would actually time our prayers with a stopwatch. This, too, served a purpose to let them know it was okay to pray in tongues a variety of ways for different circumstances.

In Conclusion

After one of our KIMI summer camps, a twelve-year-old girl wrote me a letter where she told about leading her cousin into the baptism. She shared:

"Just a week ago, two of my cousins were here from the cities. They are both girls and are our age. We were in the attic playing and just having fun when I felt led to pray for my cousin about praying in tongues. We went into the bathroom so we would not be interrupted. She said she wanted to speak in tongues, so we got in the bathtub. I told her a little about what it was like. Then I said that when we got out of the bathtub that she would be speaking in tongues. I prayed for her and felt electricity go through my arms. When we got out of the tub, she was able to speak in tongues."

I can't encourage you enough to make praying in tongues a regular part of their church experience. Our job is to train and equip our kids for the work of the ministry. Training simply means "making something (or someone) proficient by instruction and practice." Remember, our kids need to taste the supernatural, and one of the best ways is through the infilling of the Holy Spirit. As we do this on an ongoing basis, we will be helping to redefine children's ministry in the 21st century!

Taking Action

1. Have you ever led a child to receive the Baptism in the Holy Spirit? If not, why do you think you haven't?

_____

_____

_____

2. How comfortable and willing are your children to speak in tongues, and what can you do to make it easier for them?

_____

_____

_____

3. What tips can you give someone else about leading children to speak in tongues that has been successful for you?

_____

_____

_____

Lest there is anyone who may be in doubt about this whole subject, let it be known children can, do, and should know how to hear God's voice and be led by His Spirit.

Children Hearing God's Voice

Walking in the Supernatural

The purpose of the second half of this book is to help you in practical ways to take your children into the fascinating world of the supernatural in their daily walk with God. To take us there, it is first necessary to cover the most basic supernatural experiences Christians have—salvation, the baptism in the Holy Spirit, and what we are about to discuss in this chapter—hearing the voice of God. It is from these basic experiences every other supernatural event emanates.

Salvation, a profoundly supernatural experience, is first and foremost in importance, naturally. The infilling of the Holy Spirit is something Jesus Himself placed a high priority on, and we know from scripture this gives us boldness and power we need to move in the supernatural. But beyond these two things, in my opinion, there is not another subject more important to teach our children than how to hear the voice of God.

If you think it through, you will realize we can't follow God without this ability. We are crippled in making important decisions in our life if we cannot hear His guidance. I tell children regularly one of the big reasons they need to learn to hear God's voice is because someday it may save their lives! It will guide them away from danger. I would have given anything as a child if someone would have taught me how to hear His voice. I could have avoided a lot of pitfalls throughout my life, and even heartache had I known then what I know now. How about you?

But beyond that, it is with the very fundamental principles of knowing how to recognize His voice that we as believers are able to function in the Gifts of the Spirit mentioned in I Corinthians 12. It is part of being able to recognize and take advantage of spiritual dreams and visions, and for some streams in the body of Christ, it is the foundation of what they call operating in "the prophetic." All of these things are rooted in the fundamental ability to hear, recognize, and follow the voice of God and be led by His Spirit.

You can't preach under the anointing without following His leading. You are limited in effective evangelism if you can't hear Him direct your conversation. Success in healing the sick is greatly increased when you hear Him tell you by His Spirit what the root problem of their illness is. You'd better not try casting out any devils unless you've heard accurately from God what to do. To do anything effective for the Kingdom you need to know how to hear and follow Him.

My Sheep Know My Voice

Jesus said, "**My sheep hear my voice**," (John 10:27). Big sheep or little sheep—if you're a "sheep" you need to know how to hear His voice. Yet I would challenge you to ask your children how many of them know for sure they've ever heard God's voice in their lifetimes and, in most cases, very few if any of them will raise their hands. I make this a practice when I travel, and I am appalled at how few born again children being raised in our churches know how to hear the voice of their Master.

I had the opportunity to hear a minister not long ago speak on the subject of being led by the Spirit. He did an absolutely marvelous job of explaining to the congregation the basics. Then, right at the very end of his sermon, he made the most astonishing comment. It was, "Everyone in this room who's at least thirteen years of age and older needs to know how to hear the voice of God." I sat stunned. I could not believe what I was hearing. Surely, he was joking, I thought. But he wasn't.

Even though in the back of my mind, I knew few Christians gave it much thought one way or the other, I had just never heard anyone so blatantly eliminate children from the process before. Boys and girls were scattered throughout the room, and that night I had been watching two little girls in particular. It had been a long time since I'd seen children that young literally sitting on the edge of their seat listening to an adult speaker.

I wondered what was going through their heads about then.

So lest there is anyone who may be in doubt about this whole subject, let it be known children can, do, and should know how to hear God's voice and be led by His Spirit. Teach them regularly, repeatedly, deliberately, and thoroughly. Teach them early in life—the earlier the better. Make it a high priority in your children's ministry to bring them into this daily experience. I will also unashamedly say if you are not sure how to do it you need to purchase my curriculum called, "Hearing God's Voice." It contains thirteen lessons, which, if you follow the instructions, will have your children hearing from God from almost the first lesson. (Details on how to purchase it are in the back of this book.)

Calling Up Dead Spirits

One of my first experiences of teaching children how to hear His voice came through a puppet skit I had written and produced as a children's pastor. At that time, I would bring children to my house to prerecord the voices for our skits so we did not have to hassle with microphones and other problems created during live performances. I used a little girl in my group named Courtney for the lead actress. In the skit her puppet wanted to spend the night at a friend's house to attend a party, but her mom insisted she pray and listen for what God might say to her about it. The puppet prayed, and felt a "red light" (representing a negative feeling) in her spirit about going, so she stayed home. There was some type of tragedy that she avoided by not attending that night.

A few weeks later Courtney was invited to a real party by some unsaved friends at her school. She decided, like her puppet counterpart, she would pray and see if God would direct her one way or the other about going. She showed up at church the following week absolutely ecstatic because God actually spoke to her and gave her a "yucky" (uncomfortable) feeling in her heart, so she had stayed home. She found out the girls at the party spent their time calling up dead spirits for their entertainment! She was thrilled she had avoided such an event, but even more thrilled to think God actually spoke to her.

A few years after this, I was training a team of kids to do some outreaches, and part of our weekly equipping included praying in the Spirit. The kids were taking it seriously and were really pressing in. I felt impressed in my spirit that someone was to give a message in tongues and interpretation. I softly coached and exhorted in order to draw out the person who was supposed to do it. At last, a twelve-year-old boy with a quivering voice gave the tongues, and after a little more encouragement began to haltingly give the interpretation as well.

It was brief but right on. Years later when that boy became a teenager, he shared in front of the whole congregation that it was one of the most significant experiences in his life, because he was so moved that God would actually use him. I moved away shortly after that, so I was never able to take that group much further. But I had seen and tasted enough to know, yes, kids can do it too!

Your Sons & Daughters Shall Prophesy

One of the most quoted scriptures of my childhood by preachers of the day was Joel 2:28, "**In the last days, I will pour out of my Spirit upon all flesh and your sons and your daughters shall prophesy.**" In those days for the majority of Christians, even Pentecostals, the subject of prophecy was mystical and mysterious. We did not have the concept that it was ordinary everyday Christianity, and not just for professional preachers, but every believer. So whenever I heard this scripture, the hair would stand up on the back of my neck. The very thought that children would someday do something like this was profound to us. We know now that this is simply part of hearing God's voice, which is normal, everyday Christianity, yet very supernatural.

Children Prophesied Over Me

When I moved to the East Coast, I heard that there were children who were not only prophesying, but being used on prophetic ministry teams. I thought, "This I have got to see!" I wondered, "What does it look and sound like when a child prophesies?"

So at my first opportunity, I went for prophetic ministry from a team of children led by an experienced adult. At the time, I had followed another children's ministry to North Carolina who was experienced in taking kids on overseas missions trips. I was just beginning this new adventure in full-time children's ministry apart from a local church. But I had no concept whatever that I would be working for myself someday in my own international children's ministry, writing books, curriculums, and holding conferences and training camps, etc. In fact, shortly after that I was hired by another church as their children's pastor and was on their staff for another two years.

But as I sat listening to these preteens prophesying over me, they started reading into my future. I knew even then it was God, but I'm repeatedly impressed as I see what I have been led into doing since then. They primarily spoke by giving little pictures, or mini-visions, of what God was showing them. The adult was there to help with the interpretations because we were told, the children see easily, but don't always know how to interpret what they see. You will also experience this, so be prepared.

They did not speak with a religious tone of voice like adults tend to do, but very naturally shared their little pictures. The first child to speak said, "I see you as a little tiny Thumbelina, and you're sitting on a big giant egg. But I don't know what that means." Shortly the adult said, "That means you're sitting on something big, and your faith is big enough to crack it open."

One of the girls said, "I saw you writing as fast as you can."

Still another said, "I saw you talking on the telephone. It means you're communicating and getting the word out."

Another continued, "I saw a huge library with really nice beautiful books in it. I sensed God has given you knowledge and wisdom and richness. You're going to help people with everyday questions."

Short, sweet, and to the point. That's the way children minister. Don't take it lightly. They hear from God! I've received numerous other words from kids as well, such as the seven-year-old girl who boldly walked up to me after a Sunday morning children's service. Jana declared, "God told me to tell you that you won't always be teaching just kids. You'll be teaching adults too!" At the time, it wasn't even part of my thought process.

The Grass Is Greener on the Other Side

The first time we held a summer camp for kids, we trained them in a variety of areas of ministry such as evangelism, and healing the sick. Prophetic ministry was also one of them. The last night of the camp, we opened the doors to the public so the children could practice what they'd been taught during the week in a safe environment. I gathered all seventy five kids to the front of the room, sat them on the steps, wondering what would happen. This was a giant experiment for me at the time with so many kids at once. Though I had taught many kids to hear God's voice by then, it was usually with smaller groups and with kids I knew a little better.

We instructed the kids to pray in the Spirit for a minute to help them focus inwardly, then we asked if anyone had seen or heard anything. It started a little rough, and it was hard to tell how much they were hearing and how much they were making up at first. Suddenly, one eight-year-old boy raised his hand saying, "God told me somebody here tonight is going to get delivered from a devil, and it's not ever going to bother them again!"

We had pastors visiting that night, many parents who had come to pick their children up, plus many others—about a hundred visitors in all. My mind was racing. I began thinking, "Oh great! With all these visitors here?" We'd already had a manifestation of a demon earlier in the week, so I was sure he was just making this up based on that. If you were to watch the video tape, you would hear me trying to almost ignore and minimize what he said. By this time I was thinking the kids were getting way off course.

A Word for a Total Stranger

Suddenly, a twelve-year-old raised his hand sure he had something from God. "I saw a picture of a fence, and on one side it's all dark. But on the other side it's real sunny with nice green grass, and there's a man there waving his hand. But I don't know what it means."

"Do you know who it's for?" I asked

"No."

"Well, then, we need to pray and see who it's for." I had the kids bow their heads again and pray in the Spirit. Within moments, a little girl raised her hand.

"I know who it's for," she said confidently. Then she pointed to a stranger in the crowd. "It's for that man right there."

We all turned to look at a nice looking gentleman in the third row center. While I knew many of the people there that night, I'd never seen him before, but all attention was on him and his grown daughter who had been fidgeting all evening and drawing a certain amount of attention to herself. He politely smiled. Up to this point, everything had been very nonthreatening.

Almost immediately, another twelve-year-old boy raised his hand saying, "I know what the interpretation is." He continued very seriously, "You've heard the saying, 'the grass is greener on the other side,' only this time it's true. It's like being saved and not being saved. And the man on the sunny side is God saying, 'Come on over to this side because the grass is greener over here.'"

I was instantly embarrassed thinking this time the kids had totally missed it. Surely, there were no sinners in this crowd! The only people who knew about this camp were church people, and parents of the kids, I assumed. I turned to the man trying to smooth things over and said, "Well, you're a brother in the Lord, aren't you, sir?"

The Only Sinner in the House

The man became visibly uncomfortable and began to squirm just a little in his seat as the spotlight was upon him. He was at a loss for words, then finally piped up, "Well, I'm in heaven right now!"

I realized immediately I was wrong, the kids were right, and they had just nailed the only sinner in the house! I had no idea how to handle the situation, so I turned around, and we went on to something else. Shortly we began having the kids pray for the sick. Our guest speaker, Leon Kotze from South Africa, had some children and a group of adults to one side of me. I also had a group of kids with me and we were praying for someone. All of a sudden, I heard a woman crying out, and as I looked up, sure enough—we had a deliverance going on over in Leon's corner—the man's daughter!

The man was gone. He had left the auditorium and was found by one of our other speakers frantically pacing in the driveway outside the building. I never did find out who invited them, but someone told us he was Christian Science. No doubt, he had come to see kids heal the sick, was my guess, since they believe in healing through mind over matter. But he refused to talk to anybody, and as soon as his daughter was done, they left. I learned a lot of lessons that night, believe me! The biggest one was **kids do hear from God** and you better be careful because they can be very accurate!! Finally, be prepared for anything!

South African Adventure

On my first trip to South Africa, I spoke one Sunday morning in a church in Pretoria. The room was full, with about 25-30 kids and teenagers mixed in the crowd. The kids were thoroughly enjoying this newcomer with the funny accent, but it was the anointing that held their attention as I shared my vision of how God desires to use kids for signs and wonders.

As is frequently my habit, I asked the kids and teens how many of them had ever heard God speak to them in their lives. This was a well-known and respected Charismatic church in the area. Almost no hands went up. So I began to quickly assure them God wanted to speak to them. After a very brief teaching, I called any of them to the front who desired to hear Him speak to them, and the front filled with nearly every child and teen in attendance.

As the worship music played, I asked them to close their eyes and look in their hearts. I assured them God was going to speak to them. We worshipped for a few minutes. Then I began to ask if any of them heard or saw anything, and if so what He said. Quite a number of them shared, and were extremely excited because they were receiving pictures and words for the first time. There was one girl about thirteen or fourteen sitting towards the back of them who was being very quiet, and with eyes still closed, tears were streaming down her face.

I asked her if the Lord said anything to her, and she nodded and more tears began to run down her cheeks.

"Can you share with us what He said?" I gently asked.

She nodded, and through her tears she said, "He told me I must forgive those I've never forgiven before."

This alone would be a very significant word for any of us especially if it was the first time hearing His voice. But after the service when everyone had left, I was told her father had been the praise and worship leader in that church. About a year earlier he had gotten a nineteen-year-old girl in the church pregnant and had left his family and the church. God had apparently put His finger on a very tender part of this child's heart.

The Accuracy of Children

The following week I was speaking in another church where the children's pastor and my friend, Leon Kotze, had his kids highly trained in the prophetic. At the end of one of the services, I told the kids to allow the Holy Spirit to lead them to people in the congregation they felt they were supposed to minister to. They were to bring them to the front.

The kids brought a nice looking couple forward, gathered around them and began to pray. They soon began to receive pictures and words for them. But one ten-year-old boy, Birand, scooted towards me and whispered in my ear. "Auntie Becky, God shows me this man and woman are fighting in their home!"

"Well, don't say that to them!" I quickly instructed. "God is showing you this so you can pray just the opposite for them. Go back and pray that peace will come to their home. Pray that they will walk in unity, and that love will return."

So he obediently and very tactfully did as I instructed. Tears began to trickle down the face of the woman.

Later that week, the couple visited the pastor. They shared, "Pastor, we have drifted from God, but we want to repent and come back!" It turns out it was the mayor of the city and his wife. They began attending that church regularly and to my knowledge are still members in good standing. It was all because a child was trained to hear the voice of God, and spoke out what he heard in his heart.

Leon later took that same little boy on an outreach with him, and when praying for a lady at the end of the service, Birand kept saying to her over and over again, "You're sick in your head! You're sick in your head! You're sick in your head!" As the woman broke down and wept, she shared how she'd been suffering from severe depression for the last several years, and none of her doctors had been able to help her. So Leon and Birand prayed for her and she was delivered and set free.

Birand's parents told me when he was only about four years old, they were in a church service when he leaned over to his daddy and pointed to a man in the congregation who was a member of their church. He said, "Daddy, I saw a picture of that man in his house with a lady that isn't his wife. And I saw a picture of that lady over there in her house with a man that isn't her husband." The parents were understandably a little shaken, and weren't sure what to do with this knowledge. But they finally told the pastor what Birand had seen. The pastor confronted the couple and sure enough, they uncovered an affair going on in the church. You just never know what God is going to show kids, so you want to make sure you're living right!

A Teenager Rolling in the Dirt

For some reason, God seems to delight in giving children the words that can pin our adult hides to the wall exposing our weaknesses and sin. Maybe it's because when it comes from an innocent child, it's hard to ignore. We know they could have only said what they did by the power of God.

At the end of a Sunday morning service in a church in Virginia, I felt impressed to call a small group of children up to the front to demonstrate how God uses kids in giving prophetic words. I had asked one of the girls to go into the congregation and find some adult she did not know and bring them to the front. We then had this group of kids pray over them, and see what God was showing them.

The children had successfully ministered to a couple of people very accurately, even though there was nothing overly profound that took place. Then we brought the last woman up. The children demonstrated they were hearing accurately for her by giving words about her job, house, and something about her family. Finally, one of the boys spoke up. He had a very serious look on his face. He told us, "I just see a picture of a teenager rolling around in the dirt." I tried to ask him for more detailed information like was it a girl or boy, etc. but all he would keep saying was, "I don't know. I just see a picture of a teenager rolling around in the dirt."

I was clueless at what it might mean in the light of everything else that had been said. Frankly, interpreting kids' little pictures and visions can be quite challenging at times, and I don't consider myself naturally gifted in that area to begin with. But it's the position I find myself in often, and so I can usually eke something intelligent out. But this time, I was coming up with nothing. I turned to the lady and asked her if this had any significance to her at all. She just stared at me for a moment, like she wanted to say something, but didn't.

The Boy Was Right On

Suddenly, the obvious hit me, and I said to her, "Don't say anything in public that you shouldn't say."

She just said, "Okay," and we closed the service.

Because of all the other words the kids had given, the congregation had fully seen God could and does use children for His purposes, and I was satisfied we had accomplished our goal. As I went back to my book table and shook hands with people, the lady came up to me with a smile and with her voice lowered.

" I just wanted you to know that boy was right on," she said. "I have a teenage daughter, and she has turned her back on the Lord and hasn't been living right. She has been rolling around in the dirt in every way. She was here this morning, and when that boy gave that word, she started to cry."

One of the church staff members who knew the family also came up to me afterwards and confirmed the boy's word was totally accurate.

You Can Do It Too!

I've shared a variety of examples of children who have heard God's voice for different reasons, and have been used by Him to bless, comfort, exhort, heal bodies and hearts, and walk away from danger. Some may call what they did "prophetic." Others would say they operated in the gifts of the Spirit. All of it was a form of hearing the voice of God, and acting on what they heard. The most important reason to know how to hear God's voice is for personal guidance and direction in one's life. If for no other reason, it's extremely important for children to know how to be led by His Spirit. It's your job as the children's minister to train them in this life-style.

Your job will be twofold—1) to train them, 2) then release them to function. You want to always protect them. Always provide a safe environment for them to operate in. Never put them on display for wrong motives or to "show them off." Cover them in prayer, because the enemy would love nothing more than to pervert, distract, and destroy the embryonic work that the Holy Spirit begins in their lives in this regard. Give them plenty of opportunity to exercise their giftings. If in rare cases you happen to see them become proud or a little cocky over their new ability, never allow them to think they are better than others just because they can hear God's voice. Most children don't realize what they're doing is out of the ordinary and special, so it's not usually a problem unless adults make a big deal over them. As the kids become proficient and start receiving attention because of it, caution parents to protect and cover their children in prayer and not to exploit them for wrong purposes.

In Conclusion

It's very beneficial for your kids to take time on a regular basis in your services to allow them to shut themselves in with the Lord. Have them sit quietly and listen for His voice. Make a habit of it. Train them how to interpret the pictures (or little visions) that they see and even journal their experiences in a notebook. They can even receive some very profound things over each other.

You want to give them the opportunity to practice frequently, because you want to help them get comfortable with the process and become very aware of how God speaks, and how to interpret what He's saying. It's for their personal benefit, and for other people. You may want to occasionally invite an adult guest or two into your service for the express purpose of letting the kids "practice" ministering to them so their confidence can build. This is the kind of supernatural activity that kids are absolutely starving for. They are interacting with the Lord of the Universe, and everything else pales by comparison.

Can you imagine how powerful these kids could be in the Spirit even by the time they reach their teenage years if you work with them regularly? As you take your place of leadership in this arena of their lives, and faithfully disciple and mentor them, at first you may feel inadequate for such an undertaking. But know the Holy Spirit will be with you and as you teach them to hear His voice, you will be redefining children's ministry in the 21st century.

Too often we've been satisfied to hear a child pray, "Now I lay me down to sleep." But the potential of children as pray-ers goes far beyond what most of us have dared imagine.

Children of Prayer

The Potential of Children in Prayer

There is surprisingly a significant amount of information in books, tapes, videos, and on the Internet about praying children, some of which are listed at the end of this chapter. Perhaps it is because it is the one area of the supernatural that is basically an all-faiths activity crossing all denominational lines. Christians in general believe in the power of prayer, and most of them teach their children to pray on at least some level.

There are actually a number of models of children's prayer groups around the world as well that can be used as examples of how to train children to pray more effectively. One pioneer in this area is Jane Mackie from Australia. She has an amazing ministry of praying children in which she takes kids, and now teens who have grown up under her mentorship, around the world on prayer walks, and trips to train other children to pray. The Children's Prayer Network, as it's called, holds impressive prayer conferences almost every year where as many as five hundred children and chaperones fly into Australia from almost every nation on earth to pray for their countries collectively.

There are many ways of training kids in prayer. But too often we've been satisfied to hear a child pray, "Now I lay me down to sleep," or "God is good, God is great, and we thank Him for this food. Amen." But the potential of children as pray-ers goes far beyond what most of us have dared imagine. All it takes is for someone in their lives—a parent, grandparent, friend, or a children's minister—who not only believes in their potential in the spirit, but is also willing to actually invest time into their lives in training. They will see amazing results.

For those adults who have dedicated themselves to training children in prayer, rewards have been immeasurable. Such is the case with a good friend of mine, Carol Koch, who is co-pastor of her church along with her husband, Alan, in Lee's Summit, Missouri. Carol and Alan had invited me in as a guest speaker for their church and I shared many of the same principles with them that I've included in this book. She was already a committed intercessor herself when she decided to start a children's intercessory prayer team as a result of my time with them. Carol began her team the very next week after our meetings concluded.

What is exciting for me is that I am in close relationship with this church, because they are now my pastors, so I can watch first hand the spiritual development of their children. They are truly an excellent example of what God can do with a young group of boys and girls. Here's Carol's testimony in her own words:

Train By Example

The Bible says in Proverbs 22:6 **"Train a child in the way he should go, and when he is old he will not depart from it."** My thinking was, "Well, if you train a kid the way he should go, he may have a few rebellious years, but then eventually someday when he's an adult he'll come back, because the Bible says..." And this is true. But if you understand the culture of the day this was written, you realize a child became a "man" when he was twelve or thirteen years of age. They even had a setting in, or ceremony, for that.

If you study the original Hebrew word for "old" you find the word is a derivative of the word "beard." The implication is if you train a child in the way he should go, when he starts getting hair on his face and enters puberty, then he will not depart from his training." It really means, they will never leave the faith.[1]

Training means "teaching by example." So this is what we started doing with our children's prayer team. I had twelve boys and girls who came ranging in age from five to eleven. I wondered how I could pour into them what's in me about the area of intercession. I asked myself, "How can I train them by example?" I realized kids were not going to sit for an hour and a half with their hands folded and say, "Yes, Lord, come!" I knew I needed some creative ideas from the Lord.

Creative Prayer Centers

We decided to set up prayer centers like public schools set up learning centers. As I prayed about where to begin, I asked myself, "What's on our heart as a church?" I felt we should teach our children local church history, and should be teaching them the prophetic words spoken over our spiritual home and the place where they attend. I created a "local church" prayer center where I placed a pictorial directory of our congregation. I began to tell them about the prophecies that had been spoken over their church home for the last twenty years, which is what God has said our destiny is.

Then I created a center for healing because we believe in signs and wonders in our church. We believe that God still heals people today. So I got a first aid kit and filled it full of band aids. I got a bottle of anointing oil. Every time we would go over to the healing center I would train them. I'd ask, "OK, what does the Bible say about healing?" They would answer, **"By His stripes we are healed,"** (Isaiah 53:5) or "We are a people who are for signs and wonders" (Isaiah 8:18). Then I'd ask, "What does the Bible say about the oil?" This was probably their favorite thing. I'd say, "If you know somebody who's sick and you want to pray for them, anoint the band aid with oil, pray over it, and then take it to that person."

A Heart for the Nations

When our new building was dedicated, a prophet friend of ours, Jim Goll, prophetically saw two banners over us. One was for nations. One was for family. We realized we were going to have a heart for nations. So I asked myself, "How do I develop a heart for nations in these children?" By example. So I got a globe and some little stickers cut in the shape of the world. I brought in a basket and some paper. I would tell them, "We're each going to choose one nation to pray for. Ask God to put one nation on your heart. Then write it on the paper and put it in the basket." I told them, "Then every week you come in here, pray for that nation."

I'd ask them, " What does the Bible say about the world?" They'd say, "The world is going to be filled with His glory, and that He's given us nations as our inheritance" (Psalms 2:8). So I would teach them the Word in their intercession, and I have seen kids leaning over the globe weeping—little kids! We've got to train them! Train them in the things you want to give them a heart for.

Praying for Lost Souls

We also had a center for lost souls. I found a bare tree, one that had no fruit on it. I asked, "What does the Bible say about praying for souls? What does it say about evangelism?" A lot of them knew scriptures. Then I collected a whole bunch of old tennis shoes that people were going to throw away. I told them to ask the Lord to lay one person's name on their heart who was not saved. When they got a name, they were to write it on the sole (for lost "soul") of the shoe. We put the shoes under the tree, then when that person got saved we put the person's name on a piece of paper and hung it on the bare tree as fruit.

One of our main focuses here is we believe God sends people to cities. We believe God sent us to Lee's Summit and that we're supposed to stand in the gap and pray for our city. This has been our vision from day one. We believe God sent us here to pray in revival to this city and this region. So I got a big map of our city which showed all the streets. I marked where our church was and would lay it out on the floor. Then I got flashlights, and told them, "When you pray for the city, get your flashlight out and shine it on the city streets and pray, "O, Lord, let your light come!" Pray according to John chapter 1, "Lord, let your light shine. Let it shine hotter and brighter." I also got some big rubber clown ears and I told them to put them over their ears while they were praying. I instructed them to pray for the people of our city and our schools to hear the voice of God.

One of the prophetic words we'd had over our city was that this was the place of "Mahanaim," i.e. a "dwelling place of angels and men" (Genesis 32:1-2). I got some angels from a Christmas tree and sat them by the map. I told the children to ask God to release angelic activity in our city.

Growing in Depth and Maturity

That's how we started off. It was a training ground. I would give them free time and tell them to take ten minutes and go to the center where they believed God was leading them to go to, and they would. It was a scream! I should have video taped it. They'd put those big ears on and get the flashlights and shine them while they prayed. There was one little boy about five years old. I looked over at him one time and he was holding those ears those plastic ears to his head. He threw his head back with eyes closed sitting Indian style in the middle of the map. It looked so funny, but he was so serious!

Then things began to expand. I got a bunch of Bibles and a notebook and would say, "If the Lord lays a scripture on your heart you write it down. If you think God's really shown you something put in this notebook," and they would. That was the training ground and we'd do that week after week after week. But now it has changed even more, because those kids can go in the spirit instantly.

One time they were sitting in a circle. I'd been teaching them about Revelation. I would tell them "I want you to be familiar with the sights and sounds of heaven. I'd say, "Close your eyes and listen to what the Bible says." I would read to them, "Come up here and I'll show you things to come," talking about the door being open and what the streets of heaven looked like. I would read the scriptures to make them hungry.

Then I got the book "Visions of Heaven" by H.A. Baker which is about a Chinese orphanage, which had move of God about 60 years ago. The orphans in it had incredible visitations of the Spirit in which they were taken up to heaven regularly for about six weeks. I would read them the parts about the visitations in the book to make them hungry for the supernatural and the Holy Spirit. One day while we were praying, I was going through this whole process and was praying Psalms 51 about having a clean heart. I prayed that the Lord would wash over them told them to put their minds on Jesus. I told them to ask Him to show them something. Immediately one little guy raised his hand and said, "I think I see something."

I always ask them what it was in case I have to "mother" it in a different direction. He said, "Well, I saw a group of intercessors and they were laying on their faces in a circle and as they were praying it was like there was this smoke going up. As it went up, it made the shape of a key. And over here was this big door and it had a padlock on it. The more they prayed the higher the key went up. As they prayed the key went over and unlocked the padlock and opened the door. On the other side of the door was the river of God!"

Wow! That's pretty good for a little guy! Kids are hungry for the supernatural and the Holy Spirit. I have seen these kids going from praying for "boo-boo's" to praying and travailing and having this incredible relationship with the Holy Spirit. But you have to make room for them in the life of your church and be willing to take the time to train them.

Taking it to the Streets

We have a man in our church who heads up city-wide intercession. We were having an outreach one Saturday down town and he asked if I could get some of my little intercessors to pray. Only about three were able to go on such short notice, but we joined them. We followed all the adults, and we adults did all our learned intercession. It was really good and sharp, and the kids just kind of followed behind us. We ended up in the downtown area in an alley on asphalt. The adults were getting ready to finish things up, but I told the children I felt like the Holy Spirit wasn't done. I said, "Girls, come here, and let's get in a circle and hold hands for a moment and just ask Holy Spirit to come." So we did. I just said, "Holy Spirit, come!" Immediately the Spirit of God fell on them. They started weeping and crying for the city. They lay there on the asphalt with summer clothing on (it was cool out) and wept for our city for forty-five minutes. We adults did the motions, but the children actually touched the heart of God. It was amazing.

When they were done, one of the girls said, "I believe somebody just got saved." I asked. "Why do you say that?" She said, "Because I just feel like I saw an angel rejoicing. And you know the Bible says that when one person gets saved angels have a party." I thought that was amazing—she saw something in the spirit and she interpreted it by the word of God. That little girl was only about seven years old."

What Carol did, anyone with a heart for intercession can do. This is just one example of the ways children's ministry is being redefined in the 21st century. But, as we said before, this type of thing needs to become **mainstream children's ministry**. These are the activities that will capture the hearts and imaginations of our children, creating avenues of incredible adventures in the presence of God. With these kinds of experiences, we will seldom have to worry about them leaving their faith!

Kids Prayed Over September 11th

The tragedy of the September 11th destruction of the World Trade Center buildings will live forever in our memories as one of the worst events in American history. During the initial days and weeks following the event, many different people discussed how much worse the catastrophe could have been had it not been for the prayers of God's people.

There have been testimonies of how in the days and weeks before the attack, Christian groups were led in various ways to intercede for our country. One man testified of being led by the Spirit into the Catskill Mountains of New York by himself to go on a 30-day fast for the United States. A larger group of intercessors took a prayer walk up the entire east coast to pray for our country. Their efforts ended just a few days before the invasion. None of them of course, had any idea what was ahead. But I believe their prayers, orchestrated by heaven itself, were timely and powerful in protecting us from further demise. God really did have His hand on this nation.

But the Holy Spirit was at work on this situation long before the days and weeks prior to the attack. In at least one case, He began covering it three years in advance through praying children.

A friend of mine, Isabella Terry, who at the time lived in Tulsa, OK, had been mentoring a small group of children in prayer since 1998. Ranging in ages four to twelve, these children became serious about seeking the face of God very quickly. Trained to pray in their prayer languages (or "tongues" as it is also known) it was common for them to spontaneously speak English words and phrases out through the unction of the Holy Spirit. Because of this, Isabella would keep a "scribe" in the room with them. This scribe was another adult who would journal all of the English words spoken in prayer, no matter which child prayed them.

After September 11th was history, one of these scribes called Isabella and told her she needed to go look back in their journal. This person was positive the children had prayed over the events of September 11. Sure enough, as Isabella dug through the records, she discovered not one, but several prayer sessions where the children prayed in amazing detail.

Here are some of the things they prayed:

September 1, 1998

Islamic group, the chief guy in the Islamic group of terrorists, not passivists but destroyers, CIA reveal, Islamic group, blinders remove, CIA, you see, reveal, borders, border patrols, Canada, raids, search all USA borders, patrol, search, get ready, see, reveal, American 757/767, get off, back to the gate, you're grounded, air, terrorist, domestic flights, transatlantic,

India, terrorists, cities attack, USA you wake up and pray, assassination attempts, protect the president, Sadaam, underground in Babylon, underground like a city but it's underground blueprints, drawings, plans, plagues, viruses, God disgusted by terrorists, but His Hands are tied, it's up to us to pray, wake up from your slumber, you'll be held accountable, foreign invasions, Victoria, Canada, border patrol, children of Israel and children of Babylon, Hebrew, breezeways, entrances.

September 6, 1998

Jerusalem, peace, protection, the blood to cover, angels go protect, take the place, stay and protect, it's not time yet, deflect, angels protect, it's not time yet, your time has not come, Moshi, Libya, back, taking authority, the chief guy in the Islamic group, no you go back, go back, he speaks lies, stay back, Father, you reveal it, you reveal him, Syria, no plagues, no viruses, take authority, trances, go deeper, into God, healing anointing, wake up, remove the veil.

September 20, 1998

Souls, missiles, shuttles, bomb, sword, truth, divide, spirit, sword fight, out of the body, show, flow, out of the body, east coast, east coast, her groanings, east coast, the groaning of souls, out of the body, last time, from the people, they go up, east coast, east coast, last time, east coast, souls groaning, such a crying out

December 20, 1998

Terrorists underground network, sneaky, trolls, expose, water system, waterworks, see, blueprints, plans block, stop, in the name and blood of Jesus, stop, codes, conquer, punch, throw a punch, war, go, stand.

Isabella Terry shared that more recently her children's prayer team was praying about the "Burning Bush." When the session was done, she asked them if they knew what the burning bush was. They had no idea that it was the nickname many Christians had given to President Bush.

Modeling Prayer to a Child

One of the first children I ever met who was a powerful prayer warrior was a little girl named Ivy who was only three years old at the time. She first caught my attention when I visited one of her Sunday school class sessions. That particular day her teacher asked the children to open the class in prayer. Ivy was one who volunteered to pray. She began calling on heaven, covering us all with the blood of Jesus, and declaring to the devil that he was "under our feet" and couldn't hurt us. She invoked the power in the name of Jesus and numerous other similar statements. All I could do was stare at the preschooler with my mouth hanging open. I wondered where in the world that little child learned to pray like that. I had never heard anyone so young pray with such authority and use the Word of God so effectively in their prayer. But it didn't happen by accident. She had a praying mother who deliberately and strategically mentored her young daughter in prayer.

I asked her mother what made Ivy this way, i.e. if she was just born that way. It was amazing to hear the mother tell how from the time Ivy was just an infant, she had taken her into the prayer closet with her in her daily routine of intercession. As the baby grew and began to talk, the mother would draw her into prayer by asking her to join her in prayer, then guiding her, and asking her what God was saying to her heart.

When they would drive to and from town from their rural home, this mother would engage her daughter in prayer in the car, praying for everything from family issues to the people in the ambulances that passed them by occasionally. Ivy would break out into amazingly dramatic and prophetic prayers. Even when the child would play with her Barbie dolls, mom would play along with her and suddenly say, "OK, it's time for Barbie and Ken to pray now." So they would "pray" with their dolls, making it a part of the fabric of their playtime as well as their real lives. Daily demonstrating and modeling prayer, but then drawing her child into her personal prayer life routinely has paid incredible dividends in the life of this little girl, who now, at the age of ten, is a passionate little lover of Jesus.

We all know small children are little sponges absorbing what goes on around them in word and deed, and what they love and admire, they will imitate. They love their parents above all things. So how perfect it is for the parents to be the ones to model a passion for Jesus and the gospel in front of them. But it's so important not to assume they will assimilate our passions by osmosis. Children need to be taken by the hand and shown what to do in the daily routine of life. Then they can do the works of Jesus as they and their parents worship the Master together.

When the Children Travail

Probably one of the incredible examples of children being used in prayer was during the well-known revival at Brownsville Assembly of God in Pensacola, Fl. One whole amazing event was captured on a video tape for the entire world to see. Their children's pastor at the time was Pastor Vann Lane. On the video he explains what the audience and viewers are hearing in the background—the sound of children in deep travail.

He started by explaining that because of the on-going revival, most of their church members were used on a nightly basis as helpers in the services. There were multiplied thousands of people coming daily from all over the world to be touched by the revival, and everyone was needed. But their children still had homework, still needed their rest from the late nights, and so on. So Pastor Vann would allow them to stay with him in the children's room during the services for these purposes. There was a big screen in the room with a live feed from the main auditorium so they could all see what was happening in the adult service.

One particular night as the children were going about their normal playtime, Pastor Vann noticed how one at a time the children stopped what they were doing and began watching the live feed. Shortly they all began to spontaneously go into prayer. That prayer turned into the most intense, agonizing travail as the children began to wail, weep, and sob in intercession with abandon.

Stunned at what God was doing through the children, Vann guided them down the hall into an area hidden from the view of the audience. It was right next to the platform where Evangelist Steve Hill was feverishly preaching to the lost. Several ushers brought cordless mics to where the children were, and the chilling sound of their voices was piped into the main auditorium so the adults could hear what they were doing. Periodically you could hear one child screaming out, "No! No! No!" with hair raising intensity. It was as though they were crying out against abuses of others as though they were those people. The audio clip is very difficult to listen to because of its forcefulness. If you didn't know what was happening, you would be tempted to think those children were being abused then and there. Once you hear their voices, you can never be the same again. The children prayed like this for almost an hour in this manner, and it is all captured on video. Needless to say there was quite a run at the altar that night as people committed their lives to the Lord.

Esther Ilnisky in her book *Let the Children Pray* wrote:

"During a church service my husband had invited people with broken lives to receive healing. Some of those who were weeping had wept many times before, never really surrendering. Troubled, I bowed my head and prayed, "Lord, how long will it take? They should be weeping for others by now."

Then I heard a small stir. As I looked up, the children had unobtrusively moved to a wall-mounted world map. They were totally engrossed in intercession, quietly weeping for the children of the 10/40 Window."

Selah."[2]

She continued:

"Wary adults sometimes remark, 'You know, Esther, they're a little young for *that*.' By 'that' they mean deeper levels of prayer where they're exposed to the Holy Spirit in an even fuller measure that makes adults feel somewhat uncomfortable. (Perhaps those adults haven't been there themselves.) To which I repeatedly respond, 'Tell me, *how early on in life are they exposed to an unholy spirit?*'"

In Conclusion

The great healing evangelist of the early 19th century, John G. Lake, was quoted by his daughter Gertrude Reidt as saying, "Children make a sound in their travail that adults do not make. When you hear the children travail, know that Jesus has one foot in the door!"

Children are never too young to begin being trained. However, they will only go as far as we believe they can go, and as far as we are willing to invest time in their training. God needs our kids to be actively involved in His Kingdom business. We need them, and the world needs them. We must equip the little saints in prayer, and in doing so we will help redefine children's ministry in the 21st century and beyond.

Blow the trumpet in Jerusalem! Announce a time of fasting; call the people together for a solemn meeting. Bring everyone – the elders, the children, and even the babies. Joel 2:15-16 (NLT)

I dream of seeing revival spread and the
greatest harvest we've ever seen brought in
because of children operating in healings and
signs and wonders in every nation on earth.

Children Healing the Sick

It's Hard to Discredit Children

My first invitation to India had just come, and the minister who invited me was speaking out my vision boldly before I even had a chance to share with him everything I saw in the spirit for children. Victor Affonso glowed with the possibilities, "Becky, can you imagine how fast revival will spread in India if we can teach the slum kids how to heal the sick?" This was exactly my dream for the children of the world! I dream of seeing revival spread and the greatest harvest we've ever seen brought in because of children operating in healings and signs and wonders in every nation on earth. When Benny Hinn stands on TV and heals people, there are many skeptics, even among Christians, who sneer him as a phony and a showman. But when a child lays hands on someone and they are healed, it's harder to discredit.

It's been said that healing is the dinner bell to the lost. It's one of God's biggest calling cards for the unbeliever. While we adults believe in it, and know it can and does happen, it's the children walking in their infamous childlike faith who have the most incredible potential for healing the sick. The more positive experiences they have, the more their faith will build. We as children's ministers and parents need to provide as many opportunities as possible in this arena to make sure they see healings regularly. We want them to walk in greater faith than we do with more spectacular healings and miracles than we will ever see. This can happen as they exercise their faith in the same way those Olympic stars exercise their little muscles as preschoolers preparing for the day of worldwide competition. The more they do at young ages, the better they will become.

This naturally implies we must teach our children the biblical principals of faith and what it really means to believe. Even if you already feel comfortable praying for the sick yourself, I highly recommend you read books on healing by Charles and Frances Hunter. You also need to read one of the best biblically based books ever written on the subject by F.F. Bosworth, *Christ the Healer*. Read them all and teach everything you learn to your kids. Make a regular habit of praying for the sick in your weekly services and even if you are not very confident in this area, act as if you are! Believe in God and His promises, not your own ability. Just know if you will do your part, He will do His part.

An Average Sunday Morning

Nathan was about eleven at the time, and one of the members of my children's church. He came hobbling in on crutches one Sunday morning with his foot all tightly wrapped up with bandages. He was swinging it carefully in the air so as not to bump it on anything and managed to make it to the front row where he plunked down with great effort.

"What happened to you?" I asked curiously.

"Oh, I sprained my ankle and the doctor says I've gotta use these crutches for about three weeks!" he groaned.

We chatted a bit more, but then it was time for the service to begin. It was an average Sunday morning. The presence of the Lord was sweet, and as the sermon ended, I began to call the kids forward to the altar to spend time in prayer, something we did frequently. I honestly don't remember if we made an invitation to pray for the sick or not. What I do remember, though, is a group of about four or five boys going over to Nathan, circling around him, and sitting on the floor. As the worship music played, and we sat in the presence of the Lord, they laid hands on Nathan's ankle and prayed quietly in the spirit.

After ten minutes or so, I heard a familiar voice over the music and prayers. It was Nathan shouting to get my attention. "Hey! I can put pressure on my foot! I couldn't do that when I came in here this morning!"

My attitude was more of a "That's nice" response, because there are times when, frankly, you don't always know if kids are exaggerating or not. The boys continued to pray till the end of the service when the parents came to pick up their children, and I didn't think any more of it. But we were having a special guest speaker in church that night, and I had to be there early in the evening. As I walked into the building, I caught sight of Nathan and his parents going upstairs to the main auditorium just ahead of me.

Nathan did not have his crutches, nor was his foot wrapped. He had both shoes and socks on, and he was skipping up the stairs as if nothing had ever been wrong. I hollered after him, and asked him where his crutches were. He just shrugged rather nonchalantly and said, "I don't need 'em. I'm healed!"

Taking Risks While Depending on God

My team and I were on another mission trip to the Ute Indian reservation in Utah with Pastor Fred Smith. I had been ministering to his kids for a week. We kept announcing the last night of the meetings that kids were going to lay hands on the sick, so we encouraged everyone to invite their sick friends. That night a well-dressed woman came in and slipped in the back. I was introduced to her and found out she was with the Bureau of Indian Affairs in that community.

We went through the service, and I quickly briefed the kids on what we were going to do in praying for the sick. Then we made the altar call. Many people came forward including our friend from the BIA. One at a time we walked the kids through the process of laying hands on each person, praying, then speaking to the sickness or health problem and commanding them to go in the name of Jesus. Many of the people got instant relief from pain. With each victory, the kids' faith increased.

Then we reached our new friend. She told us she'd had a serious problem with her shoulder for a long time, and the doctors had not been able to help her. She could not lift her arm any higher than her shoulder and she couldn't put it back behind her without severe pain. I instructed the kids how to lay hands on her, and they followed me in a prayer.

"Quickly!" I said to her. "Move your arm and do something you couldn't do before."

She cautiously obeyed, and we watched as she slowly raised her arm over her head. Then she stretched her arm behind her back. She tested it again, placing it above her head, then behind her back. She then broke into tears at the realization the pain was totally gone, and her arm was normal once again.

What's interesting about this process of training kids to heal the sick, is many times we've seen the biggest healings when all they are doing is obeying what we tell them to do, and repeating after me. They are kids in training. But God honors His Word with signs and wonders following, and we see amazing results. Kids love being used in the supernatural in this way.

Did We Really Heal Those Ladies?

On my second trip to India, I had a similar experience in training kids to heal the sick. Actually, I only had one service with this particular group. But the room was full of adults who were curious to know if what I'd been telling them about God using kids was true. I'd taught on the infilling of the Holy Spirit, and a good number of the children received their prayer languages that night. Then I heard these unplanned words coming out of my mouth, "Now I'm going to prove to you that God's power is in you!"

I didn't say it once, but twice. My own mind was racing with, "What are you saying? You've done it now!"

But I found myself giving a word of knowledge for people who were having back, neck, and shoulder problems to come forward. About eight women came to the front including one little Hindu grandma. The last woman to come forward was in noticeable pain, slightly bent forward, and walking slowly. She was being helped to the front by a friend.

In the same way we'd done it on the Indian reservation, I trained these kids to lay hands on the sick and begin speaking to the issues in the bodies of the people needing prayer. One by one, each of the women testified of feeling immediate deliverance from pain. We got the sweetest picture of the little Hindu grandma, who could speak no English, break out into a big grin at the testing of her arm as she discovered the pain was gone. She clapped her hands to show her pleasure as she went back to her seat.

The last one to be prayed for was the woman in serious pain. The children circled around her, and we prayed. Not once, not twice, but at least four or five times before she felt any noticeable relief in her body. All of a sudden, she buried her face in her hands as the tears began to flow. The pain was gone! She stood there for a few moments weeping with thankfulness, then finally raised her hand in praise to God as she walked back to her seat without any help.

When the service was over, two little girls about nine years old timidly walked over to me with shining eyes. "Did those ladies really get healed?" they asked.

"Yes, they did!" I responded.

"Did *we* really heal them?" It was almost too much for the girls to believe.

"Yes, you did! Through the power of Jesus!"

Their eyes got big and their mouths opened in wonder as they looked at each other, giggled, and walked away.

"I've Got a Pain in my Back"

I was preaching to my regular group of kids one Sunday morning, and could feel the anointing as I taught, though there was nothing out of the ordinary going on otherwise that day. In the middle of my great exhortation, one of the boys in the back raised his hand to get my attention. I tried to look the other way because I didn't want my flow of thought interrupted. But he refused to be ignored. Finally he was almost jumping up and down in his seat to get my attention. I reluctantly asked, "Elijah, did you need something?"

"Yes!" he said. "I've got a pain in my back."

"Oh. Did you want prayer for it?"

"Yes."

I almost asked him if he'd mind waiting to the end of the service so I could finish my great sermon. But something made me stop, and my lightning fast mind began to wonder… "Elijah, when did your back start hurting? Was it hurting before you came in here this morning?"

"No," he said, "it started hurting while you were talking."

All I had was a hunch, but I decided to go with it. "Elijah, I think maybe God wants to use you this morning to help somebody else." I knew it was very common for ministers to receive "words of knowledge" about illnesses or diseases for people in their audiences. They get a symptomatic pain somewhere in their own bodies in the same place the people needing prayer have pain, but up to that point I had never experienced it myself. I turned to the rest of the kids asking, "Is there anybody else here today that has any back pain, or maybe you don't have pain right now, but you tend to have a lot of trouble with your back."

Out of thirty-five kids, eight hands shot up. I called them to the front to stand in line, then I called up Elijah. With him snapping his gum in typical kid fashion, I led him to one child at a time to lay hands on them and pray for their healing. Every single child but one claimed they had pain in their backs when they came forward, but that it disappeared after Elijah prayed for them. The only child that didn't report improvement had no back pain when she came forward, but had come because she regularly had back trouble.

Turning to Elijah after the last child was healed, I asked, "How's the pain in your back now?"

"It's gone!" he quipped and returned to his seat.

Why God chose to use one of the children that day, and not me as the speaker, which is normally the way it works, I have no idea. However, it did open an awareness in me to the fact that He will use children in any capacity He can, and we need to be careful not to put limits on Him. You never know what God is going to do in your services and who He may choose to use. I've learned when I'm with kids to stay on the alert at all times because the Lord seems to delight in doing something different all the time just to keep me on my toes! Seriously, God loves using kids in unusual ways.

Words of Knowledge and a Bunch of Kids

It's never good to assume that the Lord is going to do the same thing twice in any of your services. I try to the best of my ability to be led by the Spirit as I plan for everything, including the altar time. In the story of Elijah, God simply pulled a "fast one" on me. I was taken completely off guard by the events. It would have been so very easy to push past the hunch I had about Elijah receiving a word of knowledge in this way, because frankly, I had never heard of a child operating in that form of ministry before. Elijah was the first.

But months later, when I was out on the road ministering in another church far away, I spent some time praying before the service to see what direction the Lord wanted to go at the end. I felt in my spirit that while I was preaching that night, there were going to be two or three children who would start to feel these "phantom" pains in their bodies. I sensed I was to tell them these pains would be in places they normally never felt any kind of pain. Again, it was such a light impression it made me a little nervous. But it's all I had, so I purposed to step out in faith. I always figure it's better to err on the side of attempting to follow God, than in ignoring these impressions.

When it was time for the ministry at the end, I told the audience exactly what I had. I asked the kids, "Did any of you feel these pains?" Instantly hands shot up all over the place. I thought, Whoa! I was expecting maybe two or three hands, but there must have been at least a dozen that went up. So I decided we would go through a process of elimination to weed out the kids who had perhaps misunderstood me or were just raising their hands because the other children did.

I called them all to the front and stood them in a row. One child at a time, I asked them where they felt the pain. Each one was different—necks, heads, hearts, etc. Everyone seemed to be legitimate during my cross examination, except one. A boy about ten placed his fingers in his lower right abdomen close to his hip joint and said, "When I push right here, I feel pain."

"Ah ha!" I thought. "You shouldn't have to push on it in order to feel pain. So I think you need to go sit down." Oh, me and my great adult wisdom!

After I'd quizzed every child at the front, I then told the audience I believed every child represented someone in the audience that needed healing. I gave a call for them to come forward and stand in front of the child that represented their area of problem, because we were going to have the kids pray for their healing. No one moved. It was a Baptist church.

I explained it again and asked for people to come forward for prayer because I believed God was going to use the kids to heal the sick. No one moved.

It was tempting to believe I'd missed God, but there were too many kids standing in the front who had confidently come forward in response to my first call. So I got really bold.

"Look, folks," I grunted, "in a crowd this size, just the law of averages says that there is somebody in here that has a problem in at least one of these areas."

Finally, one at a time, people stood and began to come forward. Every single child had at least one person standing in front of them, and some had two and three—people with migraine headache problems, whip lash from car accidents, heart murmurs, and so on. We took the anointing oil and had every child dip their fingers in it. One at a time they laid hands on the people, prayed over them, commanded the pain to go, and their bodies to be healed. We asked every person to immediately test their bodies to see if the pain or problem was gone. Every person who had pain when they came forward testified that it left immediately. There were some very excited kids at that altar that night.

When the service was over, and people were milling around, a young teenage boy walked up to me with a request. "You didn't call out my problem," he said holding his hand over his right side, "but I was in an accident and I damaged my right hip joint. Could you pray for me anyway, please?

I did, then went and apologized to a ten-year-old boy.

Numb Foot Totally Healed

Here at Kids in Ministry International, we're very serious about equipping kids for the work of the ministry, to the point we have begun to hold three and four day camps and conferences to train them. In our first School of Healing for Kids we had four workshops every morning on different topics for healing the sick. The other teachers, Tim Carpenter and Lenny LaGuardia, and myself poured our hearts into the services. There were many testimonies of healing that week, but in one of the evening services, one of the little boys about eight or nine years old gave a word of knowledge. He felt there was someone with a hurt leg we were supposed to pray for.

A big man, who looked like some type of construction worker, came forward and told us about an accident he'd been in several weeks before. He'd fallen on his leg, damaged it in some way and had lost the feeling in the bottom of his foot. It was numb, and the doctors were at a loss to know what to do for him.

Tim instructed the little boy how to lay hands on the man, and he prayed boldly and confidently for the man to be healed. The man immediately testified that his foot was tingling, where there had been no feeling at all before. A few days later he came with the report his foot was totally healed.

Pain Go NOW in Jesus Name!

At the same conference after one of the meetings, a family with two boys, thirteen and nine, had gotten home late one night. Their family had been making meals for our team each evening, and so they always had a lot of cleaning up to do after the services. Tired and careless, the younger boy Andrew got out of the car without thinking and slammed his brother's fingers in the car door. Alex immediately began screaming, and Andrew and their mom quickly ran to his aid. But when they opened the door, Alex, in severe pain, began rolling around on the ground holding his hand.

"Come on! We have to pray for him, Andrew!" their mom shouted, and she and Andrew ran to his side. Andrew immediately laid his hands on Alex and screamed, "Pain, go NOW in the name of Jesus!" just like Tim had taught them in one of the sessions.

Instantly Alex stopped rolling around and sat up. He looked at his hands and began flexing his fingers. Every ounce of pain was totally gone, and when he testified at the meetings the next day, there was absolutely no sign of the accident—no black and blue marks, no stiffness, no missing fingernails—nothing. He was completely healed!

In Conclusion: It's Not About Us Anymore!

The only thing standing between children and miracles is someone who will take the time to train them. When I was on staff as children's pastor in two different churches, I made frequent opportunities for the children to pray for the sick at the end of our services. We encouraged them to pray for sick people wherever they found them—at home, school, or where ever they played.

Some churches have gone as far as having children's healing teams, and incorporating them with the adult healing teams. Some have taken children to hospitals and nursing homes occasionally to pray for the patients. If you are in the habit of doing evangelistic outreaches with your kids, you need to seriously consider allowing them to do prophetic ministry and heal the sick in those meetings. Perhaps your head pastor will allow your children some opportunities to pray for the sick after some of the regular Sunday morning services. You just need to make sure you've done your part by equipping them properly so they take it seriously and know exactly what's expected of them when they stand in front of the adults. If they are not adequately prepared for the occasion, you may lose credibility with your leaders and never get another chance.

I often tell people it doesn't matter how many people get healed because I laid hands on them and prayed. What matters is how many people get healed because of the children I trained. You see, it's not about us any more! We have a generation to raise for kingdom business.

The more frequently the kids are encouraged to engage in these areas of ministry, the more a part of their lives it will become. We want them to be in the habit of doing these things, because we want them to be better equipped than us by the time they are adults—flowing in a greater anointing than we ever dreamed of, with an outstanding track record of signs, wonders, and miracles. By equipping them in this way, we will be making major strides in redefining children's ministry in the 21st century.

Tell your children about it,
and let your children tell their
children, and their children
the next generation.
Joel 1:3

We have discovered that peer evangelism
among children...is one of the most prolific
and effective means of evangelism
in the nation.

Children as Evangelists & Preachers

Young Children Are Natural Evangelists

"Every year, tens of thousands of parents are brought to faith in Christ because one of their children was so changed by their own relationship with the Lord that the parent could not ignore the power of Christ any longer," says George Barna. "Further, we have discovered that peer evangelism among young children—one kid leading another one to the foot of the cross for a life-changing encounter with Jesus—is one of the most prolific and effective means of evangelism in the nation."[1]

In his book *The Harvest*, Rick Joyner prophesies, "One of the most extraordinary characteristics of the harvest [in the last days] will be the youthfulness of the laborers. Teenagers will be the backbone of the revival, and preteens will be some of its greatest evangelists."[2]

Young children, particularly five and under, who are raised in Christian homes seem to be almost natural evangelists. There is a host of stories of the little ones approaching a grandparent or other relative asking, "Do you have Jesus in your heart?" or something similar. Somehow, they've heard the message loud and clear that hell is awaiting those who do not know Jesus, and they become very concerned that everyone they love is on their way to heaven. As they enter school and peer influence is more of a factor, they begin to get the subtle message that it's not politically correct to ask such questions anymore, and the innocent aggression slowly subsides. We as children's ministers should do everything we can to capture this sincere interest in lost souls by children and keep that evangelistic fervor going throughout their entire lives.

Evangelism is one of the fundamental purposes of the church of

Jesus Christ, yet there are so many adults, who for various reasons, shy away from sharing their faith. Jesus made it clear in the gospels that He is not willing that anyone should perish, but that all should come to repentance (Matthew 18:14). The only way people will hear the good news of the gospel is if someone tells them.

Much of the aversion Christians feel has to do with the failures of evangelistic methods in the past, such as door to door witnessing, or the impression that we must be aggressive and confrontive with people in order to win them to the Lord. But the truth is the most effective evangelism takes place through relationships when Christians look for those golden opportunities in the lives of fellow workers, friends, and relatives when they are open and hungry for a touch from God.

Children Are Disarming

Many adult Christians avoid the topic of "winning the lost" not because they don't care about people, but purely because they feel inadequate in answering people's questions and handling any resistance that often arises. But if we can get past our own fears and aversions and remember, when children witness to their peers, they do not encounter the same arguments and opposition we get—not even from adults. Adults who are approached by children are often so disarmed by their forthrightness and innocence, they have no resistance, and their friends (other children) are the most open to the gospel of any people group on the planet! So with these things in mind, we should not be afraid to teach our children how to share their faith. The greatest hope we could have is that as they keep that evangelistic flame alive throughout their childhood, and continue the habit through their teen and adult years. In other words, in one generation we could help turn around this whole problem of avoiding witnessing if we could teach our children to be lifelong, faithful evangelists.

There are actually a number of Christian organizations that train children in evangelism. One in particular is Child Evangelism Fellowship (CEF). They even hold summer camps for the express purpose of training children to share their faith. There are also a number of curriculums that have been produced, including *The Great Commission* from Kids in Ministry International, which teach children the same thing.

Snow Fort Evangelism

When Ryan started coming regularly to our children's services at about age nine or ten, he was so quiet and reticent, I was shocked to find out what an aggressive little evangelist he was. We had been teaching on winning souls, and he took it quite seriously. His mother shared with me in the weeks and months that followed that Ryan had led every single child his age in his neighborhood to the Lord. During the winter, he loved to build snow forts in his yard. He would invite a friend over to play with him. When they crawled inside the fort, he would begin asking them questions we had taught him in children's church like, "Do you know for sure you're going to heaven when you die?" He discovered some of his friend had never heard of heaven or hell before, so he taught them what the Bible says, then led them to Jesus.

In the summer months, he would invite his friends over to play badminton in his backyard. When it was time for a break, and mom brought them some nice cold lemonade to drink, he would once again begin asking his questions, "Do you know for sure you would go to heaven if you died?" One by one each child asked Jesus into his heart.

A couple of years later, I felt led to train a group of committed kids to do some "official" evangelistic outreaches. Our plan was to go to churches in our fellowship in neighboring towns and hold a service in which the kids would do the ministry. We trained them for six weeks every Saturday morning in everything from puppetry, intercessory prayer to healing the sick. Ryan wanted to be the one to preach the salvation message to the lost.

We made him write out his sermon and preach it to us each week so we knew he had his doctrine straight and was getting his points across. We'd give him tips on how to tweak it a little, and he'd come back and preach to us again the following week. He took it very seriously. There were two or three other kids who also wanted to preach, but when Ryan did it, you could really feel the anointing on him even though he was basically reading his notes.

I coached Ryan how to give an altar call, including what happens if nobody raises their hands, and what happens if they do, what he should do next, etc. (Remember when training children, it's line upon line, precept upon precept—you need to walk them through it.) In one particular small church in Kenmere, ND, the little congregation had combed their neighborhoods and brought in thirteen kids, teens, and adults they knew were not born again. Ryan did a great job preaching and went on to ask the big question of who wanted to receive Jesus. All thirteen hands went up—one hundred percent of the sinners in the house were saved as the twelve-year-old boy preached the gospel of peace to them. The pastor of the church told us later, one of the families that got saved that night became regular attenders of their church. Ryan has since graduated from high school and is attending a Bible school training for the mission field.

Michael's Testimony

A few years ago a woman sent me an email after visiting our website. She wanted to share about her son who was being used by God in the area of evangelism. It seems from the day Michael accepted Jesus, he became a serious, dedicated soul-winner. I asked Michael to write his testimony out on paper and allow us to use it on our website. We've also included it here:

"My name is Michael. I am 12 years old and have a strong desire to serve Christ. This is because a short time ago someone took the time to the time to explain to me that Jesus Christ was crucified for my sins. Now because of this ultimate sacrifice, I can go to heaven when I die.

I was 11-years-old when I accepted Christ as my Savior. At that time I was struggling to keep my grades up in school. I had very low self-esteem, and I was always getting hurt. A few of the injuries were: A rabid raccoon attacked me when I was 5. It damaged my left calf and I had to get the full series of 27 rabies shots. I fell on a pool deck when I was eight and my wrist got caught on a metal clip. This left me with eleven stitches across my wrist, frequent numbness in my thumb, and a nasty scar. I fell on a large rock when I was nine and it went through my knee, leaving frequent pain and a scar.

I accepted Jesus into my heart on December 9,1999. At this time my family was in critical condition. My father had gotten hurt and could not work and my mother had medical problems, which kept her from working. We had no food, no oil for heat, and no hope that things would improve before Christmas. My mother had already explained to us that we were not going to be able to have Christmas that year. That turned out to be the best Christmas we ever had. After the church service on Christmas evening we arrived home to see our driveway full of toys that my mom said Jesus sent to us. There were people from our church taking bikes and gifts out of their cars. I read about God's love in that He gave His only son to die for my sins. Now I was seeing God's love represented in those people. It was then that I decided to put my whole life in His hands.

My mother got a job working in a college exposure camp for the summer. It was there that I led my first soul to the Lord. His name was Omar. He was a seven foot basketball player from North Jersey. One minute we were playing a game and the next minute I found myself looking way up into his face and asking him "Do you go to church"? He said he used to. "If you died today do you know for sure you would go to heaven"? His answer was "No." I then walked him to my mom's van and explained the Roman's road, a method used to explain salvation. (Romans 3:23, Romans 6:23, Romans 5:8, Romans 10:13) I then asked him if he wanted to pray with me and accept Jesus into his heart. We then prayed:

> "Dear Lord, I admit that I am a sinner and I believe that you died on the cross for my sins. I am calling upon you right now to come into my heart and save me from my sins. I want to live for you from this day forward. In Jesus name, Amen."

Omar accepted Christ that night and later that evening so did two of his friends.

In September my family and I lost our home due to financial difficulties. A member of our church offered us a place to stay in a low-income neighborhood across town. Even though my mother did not want to move there we had no choice. We had to sell everything we owned to raise the money for the security deposit and we moved in on September 1st. There were at least thirty children helping us the day we moved in. The children that lived here were not what I was used to seeing. These children were hungry. They ate all our food the day we moved in. My mother kept feeding them knowing we did not have the money to replace the food. She just kept telling us that God would replace it. I did not understand until the next day when people from our church began bringing over food.

I knew these children were lost and needed Jesus so I began sharing my faith with them. A week after we moved into the house my mom began a Bible study for the kids in our living room. The first week we had thirty-two kids. The following week we had fifty-four. It kept growing. I would wake up on Sunday morning before my family did and get myself dressed and ready. When my mom got up, I would grab my Bible and begin knocking on doors to get the kids on the church bus for Sunday school. My brothers would tell me I was crazy for going out alone that early in the morning in this neighborhood. But I didn't worry about that. I knew Jesus was with me.

We only lived there for eight weeks when God blessed us with a new house. By the time we moved out, there were forty-one children on the church bus on Sunday, and we now have a ministry of a hundred and forty children that my mother still teaches on Wednesday nights. Because of the amount of children attending the Bible study, we now hold it in a local church. My mom still feeds the children through donations she receives. We now evangelize the neighborhood together, and I help her teach when I can.

Since then my desire to lead others to Christ grew stronger. I now use the wordless book from Child Evangelism Fellowship (CEF®) to lead other children to Christ. I am actively involved in my church's soul winning programs. I have been accepted to attend the CEF® Youth missionary camp in the summer. I have given my testimony twice in my church. During a revival at my church in April I recommitted my life to Christ at the altar call and made a public profession of the calling God has placed upon my heart to serve him.

God will use those who wish to be used by him, whether they are an adult or a child. Many children see me as different or weird. To them I am, because I am not of the world but I am in it for now, which is where God wants me to serve him. I spend my time in God's Word, in church, in prayer and looking for opportunities to lead others to the Cross."

Child Preachers

There is an interesting group of children who seem to be born with a predisposition to preach the Word of God. During the evangelistic revivals of the early 1900s there was an unusually large number of children who became public speakers at early ages, some as young as three to five years old.

A number of children were inspired to preach under the ministry of the beloved Evangelist Aimee Semple McPherson, founder of the Four Square denomination. A minister friend of mine shared with me how her mother began preaching at the ripe old age of five after being inspired by McPherson. My friend's grandparents had been Vaudeville actors when they became Christians under Aimee's ministry. They fell in love with the colorful evangelist and began to travel with her during the large evangelistic campaigns. They helped set up her tents and equipment for the revival meetings.

One day they noticed their little girl preaching to her dollies and mimicking Aimee's preaching style. They had her preach in front of Aimee, and the elder minister was impressed. My friend said McPherson had her mother preach on stage with her during several of the revival services. Many people were saved and healed as a result of the child's ministry, which ended due to unfortunate circumstances at about age ten.

Not long ago, I ran across a Methodist missionary's website on the Internet which showed pictures of a nine-year-old boy by the name of Malachi in Port-au-Prince, Haiti who loved to preach. He and some of the children in his neighborhood went so far as to build a Free Methodist church, though it was a "brush arbor" style with mud benches. But it was none the less a church. Malachi would go there and preach during his school lunch breaks and also held services on Sunday. When the "church" was blown down by a hurricane a few years later, Malachi, who was by then fourteen, rebuilt it better than before and continued preaching.

I personally know of three children who fall into this category of natural born preachers. Two have been associated with me in my own children's ministries, while the third attends the children's ministry of a friend of mine. All of them just seem to have a built in desire to preach with no pushing, nurturing, or manipulating from anyone around them. They just love to preach and are amazingly good at it.

One of the boys is the son of an African friend of mine who I met on my first trip to Tanzania. As soon as I heard he liked to preach, we made room for him in our services while we were there. The first two times Princely preached for us, it was about what you would expect from a nine-year-old—good but not outstanding. But the third time he preached for us, he was amazing. We were fortunate to have captured it on audio tape and even have a portion of it on our website. He was incredibly anointed, and very evangelistic, and someone was saved in that service. We surmised it was the only sinner in the church that day.

Knowing He's Called

Tyson was introduced to me when he was about nine-years-old, and I was told he liked to preach, having preached his first sermon when he was five-years-old. Tyson lived a couple of hours away and only visited our church occasionally. But I had a standing agreement with him that whenever he came to town, he had an open invitation to preach for us. Tyson was actually much more of a teacher than a preacher. Small wonder, when we discovered he would ask his mom if he could listen to Brother Kenneth E. Hagin's teaching tapes from the time he was only three-years-old. Tyson was also a writer, and I asked him to write an article for the other kids one time to teach them how to put sermons together if they wanted to preach. We've included it here. He was ten at the time he wrote this:

"You have a calling on your life, and some of you are called to preach. Some of you may be called to do other things other than preach. I don't know what your calling is, but you know. If you know you are called to preach, then you need to start preparing yourself for when you are going to preach. You ask how do I prepare? How do I know what to preach on? If you don't know what you are going to preach, pray for the Holy Spirit to guide you. It is very important to prepare and some of my worst sermons were caused by non-preparation. You prepare by reading the Bible, praying, reading teaching books, and listening to teaching tapes.

Now, when I say reading the Bible and praying, I don't mean doing a word by word study of the book of Revelation or spending two days in deep intercessory prayer. Although those things are fine, they are not necessary to have a good sermon. Pray for God's anointing and guidance. When you receive God's anointing you won't necessarily feel God's power creeping over you or hear a voice speak to you, a lot of times you don't feel anything until you start preaching.

As far as teaching books, you probably don't always have the time to read large books. Good books to read, if you need help and don't have much time to read a large book, is the *Faith Library* by Kenneth Hagin. They are good books and have helped me a lot. As you read the Bible and teaching books, take notes down on paper. Use the notes to create a sermon outline.

One time I was going to preach, and I had my sermon all written out on paper. When I got up there, the anointing of God came upon me and I preached. When I got done and looked at my notes, there was not one word I said when I was preaching that was in my notes. My sermon was almost entirely different. Don't be confined to your notes. Allow God to work through you as a vessel.

What you do when you get up in front of people is a hard question. No one is totally calm the first time they preach in front of people. The thing that will probably help you the most when you're talking in front of people, is the anointing of God and preparation.

Don't think that you're not making any impact on the

people that you are preaching to. Although they may not show it, they're listening to what you're saying. I remember one time when I was preaching in a nursing home in my home town. I didn't preach very long, but when I was preaching I felt like I was preaching to a wall. Half of them were asleep and the one lady that was seeming to pay attention, I found out later she couldn't even hear that good.

Don't worry about making mistakes. They're pretty hard to get rid of. Another thing that will help you preach is memorizing scriptures. I have memorized a bunch of scriptures and it has helped me a lot. When you get up and preach, you know when it's God working through you and not your own imagination. When I am really under the anointing, I say things I would have never said otherwise.

Picture in your mind a ladder and the first rung of the ladder represents the calling that is on your life. The second rung on the ladder represents the anointing of God. The third rung represents the preparation of your sermon. The fourth represents the big scary part, actually preaching. Have you ever tried to skip a few rungs on the ladder? The more rungs you skip the harder it gets. It is the same way with this spiritual ladder you might find yourself falling off the ladder. It's pretty easy to fall down a ladder, isn't it? Every time you skip some rungs on this spiritual ladder the more likely you will fall off the ladder. But the good news is that even though you may fall off this ladder, God will gently forgive you, and let you start over again.

The most important thing to do when you're preaching is to be anointed and let God work through you. So preach the word!"

In Conclusion

It's important to recognize and honor all spiritual giftings in children such as this ability to preach. We need to do our best to encourage them to use their gifts, and back up our encouragement by actually making a place for them in our children's ministries. However, this is an area that you shouldn't push all children into. Preaching is not for everybody the way healing the sick is, for instance. We just wanted you to be aware that it exists and it is a valid ministry even though they are children.

If you happen to find you have a child like this in your ministry, nurture him and give them room to exercise his gift. But don't make a big deal out of him so that it makes the other children feel like he is more special than they are. Make sure you let all the children know they all have equal opportunity to preach in your services, if they so desire, so they don't feel like you are playing favorites. Likewise, you don't want your little preacher to get the idea that he is better than any of the other children.

Preaching and evangelism often go together, and many times the children who are inclined to like to preach have evangelistic calls on their lives. But channel them to realize evangelism is to be a part of our everyday lives, and not get trapped into thinking you have to be on stage before an audience in order to share the salvation message. Make sure that you also teach a good balance of high morals, good character, humility, and integrity to all children, but especially those who appear to be heading into some type of public ministry. As we guide and protect our children in all forms of ministry, we are helping redefine children's ministry in the 21st century.

"Behold, I and the children the Lord has given me are for signs and wonders."
Isaiah 8:18

Children and Signs & Wonders

Powerful in Prayer

Of all creatures of our God and King, children are the most naturally equipped and gifted to walk in the arena of signs and wonders because of their simplicity and childlike faith. They merely need to be told that God can do anything. Reminding them of the miracles of Jesus and the others in the Bible serves as a starting place, but I would also highly recommend telling them stories and testimonies of current day miracles as you hear about them. With the help of books, tapes and TV, there are many sources for this information, such as the 700 Club. Make a habit of writing down the ones that really catch your attention, especially ones that involve children. Then share them with your kids.

You may also want to read books to them with fascinating stories of God's might and power. Missionary magazines would also be a good source. Even something as simple as taking this very book in your hands, and reading them the stories we've included here about children will help create an expectation in them of how God uses kids. There are also other books you can read to them such as *Visions of Heaven*, by H.A. Baker that was mentioned in chapter 12 in which an unusual move of God fell on an orphanage in China. There were supernatural signs and wonders that took place for six weeks through children.

You may want to go so far as to have a five minute segment each week in your service where you tell about a present day miracle in order to continually keep before them the power of the God they serve. Remind them in their greatest moment of need, God will be there to help, protect, and rescue. Such is a story that ran on the TV program called the 700

Club. It concerned a pastor in Colorado whose house was about to be destroyed by an out of control forest fire. It was a Sunday morning, and he was called away from church because the fire had topped the hill of their property. Their house was destined to be engulfed in flames within minutes. He quickly called to the church, and spoke with the children's minister who was with the kids right then. The children immediately began to pray.

One by one each child that morning prayed for protection over pastor's house. When the fire had been extinguished and it was safe to return, the pastor and his wife drove out to see the damage. As they come up on their property they could hardly believe their eyes. Every tree, fence, and blade of grass was totally destroyed right up to the house itself, but their bright yellow house stood in the midst of destruction completely untouched by fire. There was not even the slightest sign of scorching on the outside. As the cameras showed the property that was destroyed within just inches of their house, you could easily see what a miracle it was. It was completely preserved in every way all because of the prayers of children.

Girls Raised Mother From the Dead

A couple of years ago I had the privilege of meeting a man in Africa who was an employee of World Vision. He was in charge of the relief program over children at the time, but he shared that many years earlier he had been a children's pastor. He said at the time he didn't know how to minister to kids or what he was supposed to teach them. So he just taught them everything he knew as adult about the power of God.

He shared about two little girls who came regularly to his meetings who were home alone with their mother one day. She had been sick for quite awhile, but this day she became deathly ill. In fact, she died in their presence. The father was no where around, and the girls understandably became despondent. They wept and cried for hours it seemed to them, when suddenly the older girl stopped and sat up straight. "Stop!" she ordered her little sister. "We must not cry anymore."

"Why?" the younger one asked.

"Because our pastor has told us God can do anything! We must pray that she comes back to life again!"

They began to pray when instantly the older girl found herself at the gates of heaven. Whether this was a vision or if she really felt like she was there was unclear. But as she stood at the closed gates there was a large angel standing to her side. He asked her, "What are you doing here?"

She said boldly, "Our mother died, and I have come to get her and take her home."

The angel then reached out his hand and placed some type of glowing white ball in the child's palm. Instantly, the girl was back on earth standing at her mother's side. Instinctively she laid her hands on her mom and prayed once again. The mother reportedly came back to life.

This is the only story I personally have ever heard in which children raised someone from the dead, and of course, there was no clinical proof one way or the other of the accuracy of the story. This was also about twenty years prior to the writing of this book. But the supernatural is so much more common in places like Africa, and it's not unusual to hear of these types of things. Also, because the man who told me was someone who was well respected in his area among Christians, I trusted his word enough to include it here for your consideration.

As it pertains to training and equipping children to do the works of Jesus, I am not suggesting we hold classes to teach children to raise the dead. Nor do I suggest taking field trips to mortuaries for the purpose of practicing. That, of course, would be absurd. But we do need to make our children aware that God can indeed do anything, including raising the dead. We want to set them up for the miraculous in every arena of life.

Children Casting Out Devils

Although you need to be very careful how you even mention devils and demons around children, it is a reality they need to be aware of on some level at some point. Unfortunately, we Christians have over-spooked ourselves in many ways on this subject. There have been so many books written about the powers of demons and people's nightmarish experiences, even from a Christian perspective, that many Christians are scared to death of the subject. They forget the youngest saint among us has power and authority over every demon in hell. You certainly do not want to dwell on the subject with anyone, particularly children. But I'm including these unusual stories so you can see for yourself children can function in what Jesus told us to do in the Great Commission in Mark 16:15-18— casting out devils.

A friend of our family, Paul Olson, does a lot of missionary work in both Africa and India. He has written an excellent book entitled *How to Touch a Leper,* which I would recommend you read.[1] He shares many wonderful experiences he has had on the mission field including one that also happened in Africa with children. It seems he flew into a remote village in hopes of bringing the gospel to an unreached tribe. In those cultures it is protocol to go before the chief, which is in many cases the village witch doctor, to ask permission to share your message. So Paul did this, but the witch doctor did not want any of his people converting to any other religion that would take his powers away, so he refused to let Paul preach.

However, for some reason he decided to let Paul minister to the eighty or so children and youth of the village. Paul was not a children's minister, but since it was all that was available to him, he took the opportunity. He taught the children about Jesus, being born again, and being filled with the Holy Spirit. He spent many days with them, pouring everything into them he could. All of the children received Jesus and were baptized in the Holy Ghost. When it came time for him to leave the village, he knew in his heart the witch doctor and his two witch doctor buddies, were going to be extremely angry that the children had converted.

He also knew it would be a life-threatening situation for the children, so he carefully instructed them, letting them know that the power of the Holy Spirit was far more powerful inside of them than the power that worked in the witch doctors. He wisely told them if the witch doctors or anyone else were to come after them to hurt them, all they had to do was hold up their hands and say, "I rebuke you in the name of Jesus!" He told them their enemies would not be able to hurt them.

Paul left, and sure enough, when the witch doctors heard what had happened, they began to chase the children wielding big, shiny machete knives with the intention of chopping them into little pieces. The children ran for their lives screaming along the way, when one of them suddenly remembered what Paul had told them. The children stopped in their tracks, turned in unison and held out their hands towards the witch doctors and yelled, "I rebuke you in the name of Jesus!"

Instantly the witch doctors were frozen in their tracks and fell to the ground paralyzed. They were not able to move at all until they finally declared Jesus as Lord. The last report Paul received was that one of those witch doctors became a pastor in the same village.

Though this is a subject we should handle very carefully around children, consider how important it could be for our children to realize if anyone tried to hurt them, molest them, or kidnap them that they could take authority over that demonic influence in the name of Jesus. It might be worth considering. As we teach our children how to protect themselves and take precautions like dialing 911, and never getting in a car with a stranger, let's slide one more powerful instruction in the mix—teach them to pray, "Let me go, in the name of Jesus!" It's just a thought….

Esther Ilnisky asks the questions: "Do our godly children have the right and the freedom to confront the spirits of this present darkness that are out to destroy them? In trying to shelter our children from the world, might we in reality be leaving them vulnerable to it?" [2]

Unruly Boy Delivered By Other Kids

Friends of mine in Tanzania own and operate an English-speaking Christian boarding school. It is designed for the poorest children in their country who otherwise would never be able to get a quality education. His children are all taught to love the Lord, be filled with the Holy Spirit, heal the sick, and so on.

One day a mother brought her son to the school begging Glorious to take him in. Because of his aberrant behavior, he had been kicked out of four different schools, and the Fountain of Love School was her last hope. Good hearted Glorious consented to let the boy come.

Immediately the child became a terror to the other children, hitting, biting, pinching, kicking, cursing, and in many other ways abusing them. After so long, the Christian kids had enough of the little monster. They somehow came to the conclusion all on their own that he had a demon. Without consulting any of the teachers or letting any adult know what they were doing, a group of them jumped the boy and simply cast the devil out of him. Overnight this boy changed into a model student! Glorious has since told me he's one of the best students in the school.

Angelic Drummers

It was the close of my sermon, and we had just listened to the recording of children in groaning and travail that had been captured in the Brownsville revival. Deep intercession for the children of the world fell on the whole audience for a season. Then as it subsided, and we sat in silence waiting on the Holy Spirit, a young girl quietly stood off to the side of the platform and began dancing in the Spirit. She was not disturbing anyone, in fact, she subtley captured my attention, and I just sat watching. The dance steps looked strangely familiar to me.

"Claire, do you know what you are doing?" I queried.

"No," she said without stopping.

My grandfather, who was part Native American, had taken me to many Indian Powwows as a child, and the footwork she was demonstrating was distinctly that of what one would see in the Powwow dances. When I told Claire and the group of people, we all spontaneously went into intercession again, this time specifically for Native American children that God also wants to use in this last days revival. Claire continued to dance prophetically around the room as the voices went up to the heavens.

As the prayers crescendoed, it felt in my spirit like someone needed to go up to the set of drums on the platform and beat the bass drum. I looked around but could not find the drummer from the worship team. As the impression got stronger, I finally went to the platform myself and began kicking the bass drum in a steady rhythm as much as my limited ability allowed, imitating what I remembered hearing at Powwows. Our voices and drums built in intensity until they peaked. With a defining set of thuds, I ended my drumming and the voices went silent. Once again, we sat quietly in the thick presence of God. No one wanted to move.

After several minutes, one of the people in the back of the auditorium asked, "Did anyone else hear those other drums?" At least eight to ten others in the room immediately responded that they too had heard the room fill with many loud drums at the same time I was playing. I did not hear them with my natural ears, and felt a little disappointed that I missed out on something that supernatural. It had to be Heavenly Drummers because there was no one else in the room besides us.

The entire service, including my drumming at the end was caught on video tape, and a month or so later I was editing the sermon for sale in our inventory of resource materials, and watched the entire prayer time. As I sat reliving the moment, suddenly on the tape faintly in the background I caught the sound of those heavenly drummers over my drumming! I wasn't sure if I was hearing things, so I called friends over to listen. They all heard them too. The sound of the angelic drummers had been captured on the video!

This powerful intercession and intriguing manifestation of God's presence was all because a little girl heard God tell to her to dance, and she obeyed.

In Conclusion

We share these stories purely to open your thinking to the potential of children operating in a variety signs and wonders. They are areas where we would normally never dream of taking children. Most of us adults have never done what the kids in these stories have done. Again, I am not suggesting you have classes on how to cast out devils or raise the dead in the same way we suggest teaching children how to hear God's voice or heal the sick. But just know anything adults are capable of doing, children are too. God has not put any limits on them in any way, so neither should we. Open your thinking to the possibilities of raising a generation of children to walk in the supernatural, then be brave enough to equip them. In doing so you will be helping greatly to redefine children's ministry in the 21st century.

In my opinion, it's in the preschool years that children are the most naturally sensitive to the supernatural and the voice of God than at any other time in their lives, because they have not been educated out of it.

Preschoolers and God

Preschoolers Walk in the Supernatural Naturally

One of the most frequent requests we receive in our offices is for teaching material for preschoolers (children ages two through five) on the same subjects we have outlined in this book for older children. This excites me because it shows people are not putting limits on even the smallest of our children. In fact, in my opinion, it's in the preschool years children are the most naturally sensitive to the supernatural and the voice of God than at any other time in their lives, because they haven't been educated out of it. Perhaps you've noticed how many of the stories in this book actual involve three to five-year-olds. I really believe our littlest ones go in and out of the spirit world very easily. But most of what they tell us we relegate to an overactive imagination. If we were to listen just a little closer to what they tell us with a discerning spirit, we might be surprised what we discover.

We recently published a curriculum written specifically for preschoolers called *Preschoolers in His Presence*. We took many of the thoughts and concepts that we've published for older children, and broke them down into smaller lessons, teaching only one concept at a time. We have included some of those ideas on the following pages, which if you don't have the curriculum, can be utilized with little creativity and easy preparation. The ideas are simple and yet can yield powerful results in the lives of the little ones.

Holy Ghost Learning Centers

Worship Center: We encourage preschool teachers to set up Holy Ghost learning centers in their classrooms on various areas of ministry to begin acclimating them to the supernatural in language and concept. One would be a worship center where the children would listen to at least one short worship song each week. This would not be the same as their little actions choruses, but true worship. Here they would learn to close their eyes and picture Jesus on His throne, or holding them, etc. They would learn to raise their hands to him in surrender and follow the teacher in saying things like, "I love you, Jesus."

Healing Center: Another learning center would be about healing the sick. You might have a doll in a doll bed and a box of band aids. This was a great idea I gleaned from Mark Harper's ministry years ago. Each week, place a band aid on the doll in a different place. Have the children lay hands on the doll, speak to the pain or illness, and command it to go in the name of Jesus. As they take their hands away, remove the band aid saying, "Look! The doll is healed!" Teach them to thank the Lord, and then you can go on to the next learning center.

Hearing God's Voice Center: The next one may be on hearing God's voice. Give each child some rubber clown ears and have them hold the ears over their tummies teaching them that's where their spirits are, and they hear God with the ears of their spirit not the ears of their heads. Have the children then close their eyes and sit quietly as long as possible (15 to 30 seconds for this age group). Tell them God is going to speak to them and either show them a picture or tell them something with words. After your minute of silence ask the children to share what they saw or heard. Help them "interpret" what their pictures might mean.

A five-year-old boy in one of our meetings told us when he closed his eyes, he saw a picture of himself sitting on Jesus' lap, and Jesus took a picture of him. All the other children laughed when he said that, but I jumped in saying, "Wait a minute. Why do people take pictures? It's because they want to always remember a very special moment. Jesus took a picture of Bobby sitting on His lap, because it was a special moment for Jesus that He wants to always remember."

Holy Spirit Center: Have a Holy Spirit learning center where you can tell stories about the power that comes from being filled with the Holy Spirit. For visuals, you may want to have a decorative jar of oil, an imitation fire flame cut out of red, yellow, and orange tissue paper. And perhaps some small hand-size barbells representing power and strength. Using a different visual each week, discuss with them the different things the Holy Spirit does in our lives. When you feel led, explain to the children they can be filled with the Holy Spirit and speak in tongues if they want to. Demonstrate for them by closing your eyes, raising your hands, and speaking in tongues for about 10-15 seconds. You can ask them if any of them want to be filled, and if so lead them in a very short prayer, and see what happens. Do not force anything, especially tongues. It will come when they're ready.

Salvation Center: Let's not forget to regularly tell our tiny saints about the sacrifice of Jesus and how we can ask Him into our hearts and wash our sins away. In this center you might have a real cross erected about 18 to 24 inches tall that the children can sit around. Each week teach salvation from a different angle. One week it may be His sacrifice of taking our place. The next week it could be salvation is a free gift, and hand out a little gift-wrapped box to each of them with their name on it.

Next talk about how we receive a clean heart when Jesus washes our sins away, then give each child a white heart to wear around their necks that day. Ask them if they would like to ask Jesus to wash their sins away, then pray with them. You might talk about going to heaven because Jesus forgives our sins. For heaven you could take a cardboard box, paint the inside a light blue, glue cottonballs around for clouds, and even glue some gold glitter on the bottom, and talk about the streets of gold.

Another week you might talk about wanting to avoid hell. Paint the inside of another box all black and with red and orange construction paper, cut out fire flames, gluing them to the back and sides. Discuss what hell is like, that it is a very dark, lonely place without God. One week you might discuss how Jesus rose from the dead and that's why He can save us. You can use a Ken doll, dress him up like Jesus would have looked, then lay him in a shoe box as a casket. Lift him up out of the casket as you talk about how Jesus was raised from the dead. The list can go on, but don't hesitate to repeat your lessons, as they learn by repetition.

World Mission Center: Have a globe of the world on display, and then perhaps small rubber balls with a map of the world printed on them for each child to hold. Each week when talking about a different country to pray for, bring a picture out of a book or off the Internet of children from that country. Teach the children to have compassion for the children of the world, and teach them how to pray for their natural needs, as well as their salvation. Talk to them about how important it is that we give them the gospel of hope, which is Jesus.

Evangelism Center: In this center you might display a beautiful crown with lots of gems in it and explain it is a "soul winner's crown" or what the Bible calls a Crown of Rejoicing. It represents people who get saved because of us. Also create a pair of shoes that are perhaps covered with gold glitter and other items to make them very beautiful. Tell the children these represent the beautiful feet of every person who tells somebody about Jesus. Each week you discuss how to tell other people about Jesus and why. Give each child an opportunity to "witness" to the others. For the ones brave enough to "preach" or share their faith with the others, you may allow them to wear the beautiful shoes while they are talking.

Also teach them to give personal testimonies of how God has answered prayers in their lives. Testimonies are the best lead ins to witnessing to others. Here you would also want to take time to pray for "lost souls." You might borrow Carol Koch's idea of writing the names of people who need to get saved on the bottoms of the children's shoes. Then have the children lay hands on the "souls" of their shoes and pray for the people who's names are there to be saved.

The Exception to the Rule

Knowing how busy these little people can be, four or five minutes in each center will be more than enough. But you would repeat them all again the following Sunday, or if you have limited space and time, do a different center each week. Ask the Lord for creative visual ideas, because it's the visuals that will leave the biggest impact. These activities would not take the place of normal Sunday school material, but would be in addition to it. With preschoolers, the rule of thumb concerning attention span is fairly accurate. That is, for every year old the child is, that's how long they can focus on one thing at a time. So if you have an hour class, and you can only keep your kids busy for four or five minutes at the longest, you need at least 12 to 15 different activities to keep them busy for an hour. The learning centers can come in very handy in this case.

Going back to what we said in the first few chapters about not repeating the basic Bible stories over and over again, this age group would be the exception. These children definitely need to hear them repeatedly. This is the age group (two through five or six) that thrives the most on stories. Find an excellent source of curriculum from any of the well-known publishers, and use everything they provide you. But in addition to their material, use these Holy Spirit style learning centers to acclimate your children to the supernatural workings of God. If you have preschool classes for both Sunday mornings and a midweek service, perhaps one could be reserved for the traditional Bible stories, and the other one for the Holy Ghost learning centers.

The Man in the Dark

The following testimony was submitted to us from a children's pastor in Pennsylvania who was using our curriculum called *Hearing God's Voice*. It's a report from a class of preschoolers (3 years to 5 years of age) in her church. This amazing vision is reported here by the teacher, Tina, and her classroom helper, Darrel. The children's pastor ends with some comments by the child's mother:

"Concerning Matthew's vision, our class had been going well, but up to that point there was nothing out of the ordinary happening. Our singing went better than usual as Darrel and I encouraged each child to flow by the spirit as they felt led. They all participated with great passion. Soon they seemed drawn into the worship and asked to do another song.

"I encouraged them to flow freely by moving their bodies to the beat and allowing the Holy Spirit to dance through them. It was wild, to say the least! Each one flowed uninhibited in the power of God and were not even looking at each other. Darrel and I were in awe of what God was doing. About half way through the song, Matthew looked down near his feet and shouted, 'He is down there! The man—he's down there in the dark and he can't get out!'

"Everyone looked at him and I quickly went and sat by him. His voice was strained as he spoke, and his little face was starting to turn red. He said, 'Teacher, we have to help him! He's down there in the dark!'

"I leaned over and turned off the music because by now he was so passionate about this man that the whole class was looking at him in concern. As soon as I turned off the music, I told the children to sit down, and they obeyed like I had never seen before. They all dropped straight down right where they had been dancing. The children were quiet and I told them to pray in the spirit. I softly explained that Matthew was fine, but that he was having a vision and we needed to let the Holy Spirit lead us. Each child lifted his hand toward Matthew and with closed eyes prayed in the spirit. Matthew turned to Josh, took him by each arm and said with such urgency in his voice, "We have to do something, Josh! The man is in the dark!' Matthew was getting wild with emotion for this man.

"Darrel instructed the children to keep praying in the spirit while I said to Matthew, 'We will pray and believe the man is getting a miracle! Jesus loves the man very much and he wants him to get out of the dark.' I tried encouraging Matthew that the man was OK saying we would listen to the spirit of God to tell us how to pray.

"Matthew listened to every word, even led us in prayer. But he just could not find peace. I asked, 'Do you know the man?' He said no. 'Do you see his face?' I asked. He said no. I said, 'That's OK, because God knows exactly who and where he is.' I asked him, 'What is the dark?' He answered, 'It's the man's sin. The man doesn't want to be there, but he doesn't know how to get out.'

"So we prayed that the man would repent of his sin and told satan he had to let him go. We prayed and prayed and prayed, but Matthew still was not at ease. The children all got different things as the Holy Spirit guided them to pray. It was all totally AWESOME stuff, but still the burden was there.

"It was a major move of God and even the smallest child sat and prayed showing much compassion, emotion, and concern for the man. We even used the snack prayer to pray for the man because while I was getting our food together Matthew said, 'Teacher, the man is hungry!' I asked 'What is he hungry for?' He looked at me and said, 'God!' Darrel and I looked at each other and said, 'WOW!'

Needless to say, we prayed that God would put godly angels around the man, protect him, and feed him God's word as well as natural food and that the bondages holding him down would be broken in Jesus name! Matthew told satan to 'Let go of the man in Jesus name! You can't have him!' He finally seemed to calm down after that, but did bring it up a few more times. Darrel and I told him to just keep praying the way the Holy Spirit told him to until he felt God said he didn't have to any more. We told him to have faith God was doing what He needed to for the man. Matthew looked very serious and said, 'I will!'

"He gave me a hug when he left class and said, 'I'll tell my mommy about the man!" I said, "Wonderful!' I was so blessed to be in that day! The entire experience of teaching this and watching all that God is doing is life changing and so exciting!"

Children's pastor's closing comments:

Matthew was encouraged to go home and tell his mom about what happened in class but he never did, so she didn't know about the vision. But later that day he told his mom he had a "word." His mom asked, "What is the 'word'?" He told her, "The man is going to be OK." His mom didn't know what he was talking about and asked him about the man. He would only repeat with great passion that the man was OK! When I talked with her later, I told her what her son had experienced in class. She then understood what the "word" was connected to.

Beatrice

The first time Beatrice came to my attention was during a worship conference in North Carolina. She was only four years old at the time. It had been a powerful conference, and this particular night, the song leader was inviting people from the congregation up to the front to sing the spontaneous song of the Lord in the microphone while the worship band played. A big long line of people went to the front, and at the end of the line, so short she almost wasn't seen, was Beatrice. It took quite awhile for all of the people ahead of her to get done with their turns, but she waited very patiently never leaving the line as most other preschoolers might have done.

Beatrice was the very last one in line to have a turn when the song leader smiled and handed her the mic. She jumped smoothly into the song, and began singing spontaneous melodies and lyrics by the Spirit of God. She was on pitch and in perfect rhythm with the musicians. She sang words far beyond her years of knowledge and experience as she began to declare the destinies of the children in the kingdom. I was stunned.

In another incident, Beatrice was with her dad and grandfather one afternoon playing on a big swing set at a park. Her dad was swinging her really high for such a little girl, and her grandfather asked, "Beatrice, aren't you afraid of swinging so high?"

"Nope!" she said confidently.

"Why not?"

"Because there's a big angel over there watching out for me!"

You Will Live and Not Die!

One of my hobbies, if you will, is to collect video and audio tapes of children doing profound things for God, whether it's healing the sick, praying, dancing, preaching, or worshiping. One tape that was sent to me involved a precious four-year-old boy named Joshua. Joshua and his family had been a part of a church in California before going to Ireland as missionaries.

While in Ireland, they received word that Joshua's children's pastor back in the states had become gravely ill due to her pregnancy and was not expected to live. Actually, by the time they received the message, she was already considered clinically brain dead.

But the minute Joshua heard the news he immediately wanted to fast and pray for her.

His parents set up a little cassette player for him, and he taped a prayer for his teacher, which they then sent to her. In the taped message, he told her he wanted to thank her for helping him get filled with the Holy Spirit, because, "I really use that Holy Spirit to help my dad at the altar." He shared some other things about his baby sister, then he prayed. The prayer was very short but powerful. In it he said, "I speak to that blood clot in Chia's head and command it to go in Jesus name." He prayed for her protection with the blood of Jesus and prayed that she would live and not die, and be able to raise her little baby. It was a very mature prayer for such a little guy, and Chia did live to raise her baby girl. Even the doctor's report declared it a miracle.

The Adventures of Ivy and God

Ivy was the little girl the church where I was the children's pastor whom I spoke of in the chapter on children and prayer. Though Ivy was too young to be in my children's services while I was there, her mother would keep me informed about her daughter. These stories and others have been a great source of inspiration to me, and for years have fostered my belief that preschoolers can be powerful ministers.

Grandpa's Eyes

Two-year-old Ivy's grandpa had suddenly developed some serious eye problems—detached retinas, the doctor said. Surgery offered only a 50/50 chance of improvement, but her grandpa decided it was his only hope of seeing normal again, so he went for it. As far as the doctor could tell, the procedure had been a success, but for some reason her grandpa's eyes simply were not healing. Strong light had become blinding and he had to wear special sunglasses that framed all sides of his eyes to keep out the unpleasant rays. Two months had passed with no improvement.

He went over to Ivy's to visit one afternoon, noticeably discouraged. There wasn't a lot that could be said to encourage him, and finally he got up to leave. Once he was gone, Ivy came running from her bedroom to her mother and asked, "Where's grandpa?" "He just left," her mom said, when Ivy nearly shouted, "No!" and ran outside to catch him.

"Grandpa! Grandpa! Wait! I have to do something!" she hollered running down the sidewalk. Grandpa patiently bent down, picked her up, and said, "What do you have to do?"

"I have to kiss your eyes!" and with that she removed his glasses and kissed each one of his eyes and said, "Jesus!" She then put the glasses back on his face. Once she was done, she jumped out of his arms and went back into the house to play. Within a week, grandpa's eyes were totally healed and he was able to go back to work.

Standing in the Gap at Age Two

Ivy's mom didn't quite know what to think at first when her two-year-old daughter bent over and started to wail loudly in what seemed to be some type of intercession. It looked so funny, it was all mom could do to keep from laughing. She asked Ivy what was wrong, and all Ivy could say was "Rachel," which was the name of another two-year-old in our church. So finally the mother told Ivy, "You just pray the best you can and I'll pray in my prayer language," which she did.

A couple minutes later, Ivy suddenly stopped and said, "All done!" and jumped down from where she had been sitting and ran off to play.

Ivy's mom didn't think any more of it until the next day when she was visiting with Rachel's mom, Julie.

Julie started telling how she thought she was going to have to take Rachel to the emergency ward the day before because she had stuck a bead up her nose and they couldn't get it out. The little girl didn't know how to blow it out and instead kept inhaling it deeper. But finally after much work they got it out. The mothers compared the time periods between the incident and when Ivy had gone into prayer, and they were within an hour or so of each other.

Prophetic Bike Riding

Learning to ride her bicycle without the training wheels had become a passion with four-year-old Ivy, and for those of us who knew her, we could vouch for the fact that she's not one to give up easily. But none the less, after struggling all day long and into the evening, even with daddy's help, she just couldn't quite get the hang of it. She finally went into the house for supper, defeated for the day.

Ivy was worn out from trying so hard. As she sat down to a bowl of Cheerios (a type of breakfast cereal) for supper that night, she occasionally dozed off for a minute, just long enough for a Cheerio or two to drop out of her mouth.

Then with an unexpected bolt of energy, Ivy shot out of her chair shouting, "Mom! Mom! Jesus just showed me how to ride my bicycle! Do you think Daddy will help me try one more time tonight?" she asked, and with mom's approval, Ivy ran outside. A few minutes later her mother went to check on her daughter, and there she was riding just as big as you please all the way down the sidewalk on her two-wheel bike.

"What happened?" the mother asked. Ivy's dad replied "I don't know. She just came out and started riding with no trouble!"

Earthly Treasures

Driving home one night from church, an ambulance passed by the family car. Ivy's mother said, "Let's just pray for whoever is in that ambulance." It was a rather uneventful prayer followed by silence, when all of a sudden Ivy began again. She began praying about the man in the ambulance that he would be made whole and "That he would come to know you, Lord, and that the sickness wouldn't take him."

Ivy's mother, not wanting to break in on the moment, just began praying in the Spirit with her daughter, when Ivy exploded.

"Yes, and that Chinese family, that they would come to know you, Lord, the whole family, and that they would be free!" The four-year-old then began rebuking the devil, and it was all the mother could do to keep from laughing as her daughter began calling the devil names.

"You big stinky thing!" she hollered, "And yes, you're a god, but you're not my god! You're the god of this world, but I don't serve you like some people do !"

Mom wasn't laughing anymore. She was thinking, "Who taught her that? I didn't teach her those things."

As they pulled into the family driveway, Ivy began slowing down. The peace of God visibly settled upon her. She was holding a little box full of her favorite toys that she loved very much. She looked at them and said to her mom, "I don't need these anymore. I've got Jesus! Let's give them away." Mom wisely guided her with, "You know that happens when you get close to God. Possessions don't mean as much to us. You realize you heart's not in these things like it used to be. But let's don't give them away yet, let's think about it for a little while." Ivy listened to her mom and with that they were in the house.

Hamburger Intercession

Burger King Restaurant seemed like an unlikely place for anything spiritual to happen, but while Ivy's family stood in line to order their meals, her mom, struck up a simple conversation with the people behind them. The woman was pregnant, Ivy's mom asked the typical questons you ask a mother-to-be, picked up her food, and they went to their table to eat.

They sat down, and the woman and her family sat behind them, ate their meal with no further incident and eventually stood up to leave.

Mom noticed Ivy watching them out of them corner of her eye. Quietly the four-year-old set her hamburger down on the table, and just stared at her food. Mom knew her daughter well and asked, "What's going on in here, Ivy?" as she placed her hand over her own stomach. "Do you feel like you need to pray?"

Ivy nodded her head and took off with her typical blow-you-away prayer power and began pleading the blood of Jesus over that family. She prayed things like, "and that car will not hit them and they will make it all the way home in Jesus' name!"

With that, the child picked up her hamburger and finished her meal. Later, mom nonchalantly asked her daughter, "So did you feel like a car was going to hit those people?

"Yep!" Ivy answered, "but not any more!"

"Children often don't know why they feel an urgency to pray," says Esther Ilnisky of the Global Children's Prayer Network. "They just do; so give them room, just let them. Allowing them to pray, to express themselves toward God, could abort a tragedy that we can't see coming our way."[1]

In Conclusion

There are so many other stories about preschoolers, which could be included, but these will hopefully open your minds and hearts to know that God can and does powerfully use preschoolers for His purposes. What an army for God we would have if we could catch a vision for raising our children from the womb to serve their Master all the days of their lives. This is a message that must spread far and wide, and not just to children's ministers, but parents and grandparents as well. If we start our children in the supernatural when they are young, and keep training them all the days of their lives to do the works of Jesus, we will most definitely redefine children's ministry for the 21st century.

These are concepts that must be incorporated into mainstream children's ministry if we are going to stem the tide of evacuation of our young people from the church as they enter adulthood.

Final Thoughts

The ideas presented in this book may be completely new to you as it relates to children's ministry. If so, it may be a lot to digest at one time. We have made a list below to help summarize the main points we've stressed as areas needing change. If we are going to capture the hearts and imaginations of our children with greater hope of keeping them as active members of the church of Jesus Christ, these are the areas that need our most prayerful consideration. These are concepts, based on my personal experiences and viewpoints as a children's minister, that must be incorporated into mainstream children's ministry if we are going to stem the tide of evacuation of our young people from the church as they enter adulthood. I've seen them work through my years of ministry. There are many other voices in children's ministry that may have varying perspectives. They are all worthy of consideration. But to me, these are the real fundamental issues that can be used in any type of ministry or parenting of children.

1. We must remember children need their own personal experiences and encounters with the living God. We must also embrace the fact they are capable of experiencing anything and everything God makes available to us as spiritual beings. Therefore we must make every effort to see that God is tangibly present in every children's service. We do this by setting apart times of genuine worship, taking them into the very throne room of heaven, allowing for times of sitting quietly in His presence listening for His voice then sharing with each other what we see and hear. It also happens when we provide times at an old-fashioned altar where kids are encouraged to seek His face regularly.

2. We need to seriously reconsider the spiritual menu and diet we feed our children on. We must realize they are very capable of handling the "meat" of the word, i.e. topics normally considered proper for adults only. We need to realize that even what the Bible identifies as "milk" is much meatier than what we typically feed our children. We must get off the treadmill of feeding our kids a continual diet of basic Bible stories with little to nothing else in the mix, and make sure they are grounded in all of the basic Bible doctrines and concepts that cause us to lead supernatural, victorious lives.

3. As both children's ministers and parents we must adjust our teaching styles to include active, deliberate, on-purpose, hands-on mentoring in all areas where Christians need to be discipled. We need to recognize our job is to train and equip the little saints, which means not just telling them how to do the works of Jesus, but actually showing them, then giving them opportunities to practice and do what we've shown them. Our children's ministries must become clinics of functioning Christianity in all areas of the believer's ministry. This includes healing the sick, hearing His voice, being led by the Spirit, prayer and intercession, worship, soul-winning, preaching, signs and wonders, operating in the gifts of the Spirit, prophetic ministry, and anything else Jesus considered normal Christianity.

4. We need to get a fresh vision of what it is we are called to. We must ask ourselves what a child who is a committed follower of Jesus looks like, and what it will take to get him/her there. It will take a completely different approach to teaching children than we are presently using. It needs to include actively doing the works of Jesus. It should be just as common to hear a church has a children's prayer team, a children's healing team, a children's prophetic ministry team, and a children's evangelism team as it is to hear they have a Sunday School. Our fresh vision of what we are called to should embrace equipping children to function in the believer's ministry.

5. Church leaders, specifically fivefold ministers, need to se-

riously reconsider their role to the health and vitality of the children under their leadership, and not be content to completely delegate all contact and input to the children's ministers and workers under them. They need to recognize as true fivefold gifts to the body that they can release and activate things in the children and teens of their churches that no one else can. Head pastors, elders, and board members need to recognize it is as vitally important to place fivefold ministers over their children's ministries as it is to place them over the adults. Those who believe they are called into full-time ministry as true apostles, prophets, evangelists, pastors, and teachers need to seriously seek God to determine if they are in fact called to children's ministry rather than adult ministry. The reason is because there is a serious disproportion of laborers in the vast field of children in comparison to the number of children and youth needing to be reached. Pastors and other ministers need a serious attitude adjustment in regards to ministry over children seeing it as critical to the healthy survival of the Church at large.

6. There must be a fresh partnership between parents and the church, where the church must help educate and equip parents how to disciple, and equip their children at home. We as church leaders must give them the tools, confidence, and understanding to continue the spiritual process in the daily lives of their children, which the church cannot do. We begin by helping parents see the potential of their children. We must show them how they can help their children walk in the supernatural at home, school, and play, not just at church. We must help them begin to think in terms of true discipling and mentoring in the home, which will more than likely include training the parents as well.

7. We must see gifted, anointed, trained musicians look seriously at their roles in children's ministry to take our children to the highest levels of praise and worship, which is vital to our Christian walk. Rather than seeing praise and worship for children as low-level worship, we need to help musicians realize how intensely children can worship when trained and given the opportunity. We need to pray for God to send musical laborers into the fields of children to catapult them to greater levels of heavenly throne room experiences.

8. We need to once again get serious about bringing our children into the fullness of the Holy Spirit, including speaking in tongues to lay the foundation for a supernatural life in Christ. We need to present it to them often and regularly, but clearly teaching them why it is valuable, and what this experience will do for them in their Christian walk. We must help train and disciple them to use their new gift during our services frequently to get them in the habit of incorporating it into their lives. If we don't we risk the chance, they will have a one time experience of speaking in tongues, and possibly never use it again.

9. It is critically important we teach our children how to hear and recognize the voice of God, and how to obey and follow His leading. This training should start as early as preschool and continue throughout their lives. We believe that next to salvation and the baptism in the Holy Spirit, training children to hear God's voice is the most important thing we can teach them.

10. To truly redefine children's ministry in our lifetime worldwide, it is critical that this message be presented not only to children's ministers, but also to church leaders, parents, publishers of children's curricula, authors of children's books, producers of children's music, videos, DVDs, and all other resource materials and products created for our Christian children. This includes educating Christian bookstore owners, television show producers, Bible schools and colleges, training and equipping centers, missionaries, and church planters, and anyone else connected with educating church leaders. We all need radical changes in our thinking and actions in order to change the face of ministry to children and reverse the trend of the massive drainage of our young people out the back door of the Church.

Does It Really Work?

The first group of kids I ever pastored were with me for eight years. Though I was still young and inexperienced in children's ministry in the early days, I still endeavored to teach them nearly everything I have outlined in this book as much as I knew to do. Many of the stories included here come from those early days.

As the years went by, the youth pastor of the church often told me that each year kids graduated out of our children's ministry into his youth group, he noticed each succeeding class was that much spiritually stronger than those that had preceeded them. Several years after I had moved away, I was told from people who still attended the church, that the last of my group of kids was graduating from high school. The youth leader had told them that as long as my kids were in his group they experienced revival, growth, and kids who were on-fire for God. Then he added an interesting comment. He said the group of kids coming after them, who had not sat under my ministry, were just the opposite.

So the question is, does it work? I can only speak from personal experience and say unequivocally and resoundingly, "Yes!"

With confidence I can prophesy if we do all of these things, we will definitely redefine children's ministry in the 21st century and beyond, and make radical changes in the body of Christ in many ways. We will help Jesus in His yet unfulfilled desire to gather the children of the world unto Himself and the Church will be infinitely stronger and more powerful than we've yet seen in our history!

Get up! Cry out at night, every hour on the hour. Pour your heart out like water in the presence of the LORD. Lift up your hands to him [in prayer] for the life of your little children who faint from (spiritual)* hunger at every street corner.

Lamentations 2:19 (GWT)

* (My insert)

Becky Fischer
Founder/Director of Kids in Ministry International, Inc.

About the Author

Becky Fischer, a children's pastor since 1991, grew up in a traditional Pentecostal church environment. Having received Jesus as Savior and the infilling of the Holy Spirit at an early age, she knows first hand that children can be both touched and used by God. Becky spent twenty three years in business before answering the call to full time ministry.

During the last eight of those years, Becky spent her spare time as the children's pastor in her local church, Word of Faith Church and Outreach Center in Bismarck, ND. She later moved to North Carolina to join Tasch Ministries International, a ministry that had at that time taken over 700 boys and girls on missions trips. She was then asked to be the children's pastor of a new church plant in Wilkesboro, NC by MorningStar Publications and Ministries, Inc. under Rick Joyner (now called MorningStar Fellowship Church). She also worked part time in the publications department of MorningStar as a graphic artist and still is a contributing author to the MorningStar Journal.

Becky founded Kids in Ministry International in 2001. Since that time she has dedicated her full time to writing and publishing, as well as teaching in churches and conferences, traveling overseas training others to work with children. Kids in Ministry International, now with addtional bases in three other nations (Mexico, India, and Kenya), holds annual KIMI camps, conferences, and seminars.

During the 2006 Asuza Street Centennial Celebration in Los Angeles, CA, Becky was one of only seven children's ministers worldwide invited to be a workshop speaker. She and her ministry recieved nationwide attention as the focus of a documentary film called *Jesus Camp* that was nominated for an Oscar Award in 2007.

As an author, she has written numerous curricula specially designed for children to have a supernatural encounter with God. Becky pastors a church in Mandan, ND called the Fire Center, an unusual church plant with a focus on kids and teens.

Notes

Chapter One

1. *Real Teens*, George Barna, Regal Books, Ventura, CA, copyright © 2001, pg 136
2. Encyclopedia of Religion and Society, Dr. William H. Swatos, Religious Education, Hartford Institute for Religion Research, Hartford Seminary, 77 Sherman Street, Hartford, CT 06105
3. *Transforming Children into Spiritual Champions,* George Barna, copyright © 2003, Issachar Resources, Ventura, CA, pg 41
4. Reprinted with permission from *Ministries Today*, May/June 2004. Copyright Strang Communications Co., USA. All rights reserved. www.ministriestoday.com
5. *Transforming Children into Spiritual Champions,* George Barna, copyright © 2003, Issachar Resources, Ventura, CA, pg 65
6. *Let the Children Pray*, Esther Ilnisky, copyright © 2000, Regal Books, Ventura, CA, pg 41

Chapter Two

1. *Transforming Children into Spiritual Champions*, George Barna, copyright © 2003, The Barna Group, Ventura, CA
2. *Kids Making a Difference*, Pete Hohmann, copyright © 2004, This book is a collection of incredible stores of what kids today are doing around the world. Order from Gospel Publishing House, Item # 03TW6353. Go online at www.gph.org or call 1-800-641-4310 or 417-862-2781 ext 4009 (outside the US).
3. Definition for *"Tweener"*: a modern term for children between the ages of 8 and 12.
4. *Children Aflame*, David Walters, copyright © 1995, Faith Printing Company, pg 40
5. *Real Teens*, George Barna, copyright © 2001, Regal Books, pg 115-116

Chapter Four

1. *Teaching Cross-Culturally*, Judith E. Lingenfelter, Sherwood G. Lingenfelter, Baker Academic, Grand Rapids, MI, © 2003, page 27

Chapter Five

1. *Eli! Eli! I'm Calling You to Children's Ministry!* Pamela Ayres, Hansel & Gretel Ministries, copyright © 2003, Moravian Falls, NC

Chapter Six

1. *Transforming Children into Spiritual Champions,* George Barna, copyright © 2003, Issachar Resources, Ventura, CA, pg 111
2. Ibid., pg 111
3. Ibid., pg 111
4. Ibid., pg 109
5. Ibid., pg 110

Parental Resources:
Raising a Forerunner Generation, Lelonie Hibberd, Kingsgate Publishing, 1000 Pannell Street, Suite G, Columbia, MO 65201
Spiritually Parenting Your Preschooler, C. Hope Flinchbaugh, Charisma House, 600 Rinehart Road, Lake Mary, FL 32746
An Introduction to Family Nights, Jim Weidmann & Kurt Bruner, Cook Communications Ministries, 4050 Lee Vance View, Colorado Springs, CO 80918
Parents' Guide to the Spiritual Growth of Children , Focus on the Family, Colorado Springs, CO 80995

Chapter Nine

Suggested Reading:
Ten Reasons Why Every Believer Should Speak in Tongues by Kenneth E. Hagin, Kenneth Hagin Ministries, PO Box 50126, Tulsa, OK 74150-0126

Chapter Twelve

1. *(Root word "zaqen" [2204 Strong's Concordance] is the word for Old. A derivative of it "Zaqan" [2206 Strong's Concordance] is word for "beard."*
2. *Let the Children Pray,* Esther Ilnisky, copyright © 2000, Regal Books, Ventura, CA, pg 135
3. Ibid., pg 37

Website for involving children in prayer:
PrayKids: http://www.navpress.com/Magazines/PrayKids!
Presidential Prayer for Kids, or http://www.pptkids.org/index.php
Kids Prayer Network: http://www.kidsprayer.com

Contact Kids in Ministry International for the following recommended resources by visiting our online bookstore at www.kidsinministry.com or calling 701-258-6786:

Books: *Reconnecting the Generations,* Daphne Kirk
       Let the Children Pray, Esther Ilnisky
       Raising Your Children for Christ, Andrew Murray
       Visions of Heaven, H.A. Baker
       Equipping a Generation to Pray Manual, Carol Koch

DVDs: *Raised Up & Set Apart,* Becky Fischer
       School of Healing Conference for Kids, Becky Fischer

CDs: *Changing the World Through Prayer CD Series,* Becky Fischer
       Extreme Makeover Conference, Becky Fischer
       Children and Listening Prayer, Kathleen Trock

Chapter Fourteen

1. *Transforming Children into Spiritual Champions,* George Barna, copyright © 2003, Issachar Resources, Ventura, CA, pg 68
2. *The Harvest,* Rick Joyner, copyright © 1993, Whitaker House, New Kensington, PA, page 34, Excerpts used by permission. For more information: www.morningstarministries.org

Chapter Fifteen

1. *How To Touch a Leper,* Paul R. Olson, copyright © 1986, New Day Publishing Company, Mound, MN, chapter 6, pg 85
2. *Let the Children Pray,* Esther Ilnisky, copyright © 2000, Regal Books, Ventura, CA , pg 36

Chapter Sixteen

1. *Let the Children Pray,* Esther Ilnisky, copyright © 2000, Regal Books, Ventura, CA, pg 45

Finally! Something deep for Kids!

Children's Church Curriculum
for your children's church, Sunday School, or home school.
(For ages 6-12)

Our Amazing God
Seventeen lessons covering important biblical foundations including the Trinity, Salvation, Water Baptism, Baptism in the Holy Spirit, and spirit, soul, and body. You've never seen it taught this way before!

Hearing God's Voice
A tremendously easy to understand course of thirteen lessons teaching children how to hear the voice of God, be led by His Spirit, and begin operating in the prophetic. Even adults say they learn a great deal from this series!

The Great Commission
Take advantage of your children's natural evangelistic tendencies teaching them what the Bible has to say about winning the lost. Also included is a helpful training manual to activate your children in evangelism in their everyday lives.

The Blood of Jesus
Take your children on a journey through the entire Bible following the "scarlet thread," i.e. nearly everything the Word has to say on the topic of the blood of Jesus. Extremely foundational for every believer!

To see more details on each curriculum as well as sample chapters, visit our website at www.kidsinministry.com.

For more information, contact:
Kids in Ministry International
511 S. Anderson St. * Bismarck, ND 58504
Call 701-258-6786 or email:
kidsinministry@yahoo.com
Visit us online at www.kidsinministry.com